A Custom Edition for The Art Institute Online

AESTHETICS

A Reader in Philosophy of the Arts

Printed in the United States of America

10 9 8 7 6 5 4 3 2 1

ISBN 0-536-20158-7

2006440011

RG/AR

Please visit our web site at *www.pearsoncustom.com*

PEARSON CUSTOM PUBLISHING
75 Arlington Street, Suite 300, Boston, MA 02116
A Pearson Education Company

COPYRIGHT ACKNOWLEDGMENTS

Grateful acknowledgment is made to the following sources for permission to reprint material copyrighted or controlled by them:

"Against Imitation" and "Allegory of the Cave," excerpted from "The Republic," by Plato, reprinted from *The Dialogues of Plato* 1, translated by Benjamin Jowett, (1892).

"The Limits of Likeness," by Ernst Gombrich, reprinted from *Art and Illusion*, (1956), by permission of Princeton University Press. Copyright © 1969 by the Trustees of the National Gallery of Art.

"Reality Remade," by Nelson Goodman, reprinted from *Languages of Art*, (1968), by permission of Hackett Publishing Company, Inc.

"The Work of Art in Age of Mechanical Reproduction," by Walter Benjamin, reprinted from *Illuminations*, translated by Harry Zohn, (1955), Harcourt Inc.

"Why Photography Is Not Art," by Roger Scruton, reprinted from *The Aesthetic Understanding*, (1983), Routledge.

"What's So Special About Photography?" by Ted Cohen, reprinted from the *Monist*, (April 1988).

"The Power of Movies," by Noel Carroll, reprinted from *Daedelus* 114, no. 4 (fall 1985), by permission of MIT Press Journals. Copyright © 1985 by the American Academy of Arts and Sciences.

"The Expression and Arousal of Emotion in Music," by Jenefer Robinson, reprinted from the *Journal of Aesthetics and Art Criticism*, winter 1994, Blackwell Publishing, Ltd.

"Representation in Music," by Roger Scruton, reprinted from *The Aesthetic Understanding*, (1983), Routledge.

"Beneath Interpretation," by Richard Shusterman, reprinted from *Pragmatist Aesthetics*, (1992), Blackwell Publishing, Ltd.

"What Is Going On in a Dance?" by Monroe C. Beardsley, reprinted from *Dance Research Journal*, no. 15 (1982).

"Televison and Aesthetics," excerpt from "Innovation and Repetition: Between Modern and Post-Modern Aesthetics," by Umberto Eco, reprinted from *Daedulus* 114, no. 4 (fall 1985), by permission of MIT Press Journals. Copyright © 1985 by the American Academy of Arts and Sciences.

"Adorno's Case Against Popular Music," by Lee B. Brown, reprinted from *Aesthetics: A Reader in Philosophy of the Arts*, First Edition, edited by David Goldblatt and Lee B. Brown, (1996), by permission of Prentice-Hall, Inc.

"Jokes," by Ted Cohen, reprinted from *Pleasure, Preference and Value*, edited by Eva Schaper, (1983), Cambridge University Press.

"Pornography," by Joel Feinberg, reprinted from *Offense to Others: The Moral Limits of the Law* 2, (1988), by permission of Oxford University Press, Inc. Copyright © 1988 by Oxford University Press, Inc.

Excerpt from *Art As Experience*, by John Dewey, (1934), Putnam Publishing Group.

"The Role of Theory in Aesthetics," by Morris Weitz, reprinted from the *Journal of Aesthetics and Art Criticism*, September 1956, Blackwell Publishing, Ltd.

"Are Art Museums Racist?" by Maurice Berger, reprinted from *Art in America*, September 1990.

"On the Concept of Music," by Jerrold Levinson, reprinted from *Music, Art, and Metaphysics*, (1990).

"Virtual Space" and "Virtual Powers," by Suzanne Langer, reprinted from *Feeling and Form*, (1953), Allyn and Bacon.

"Architecture as Decorated Shelter," by Robert Venturi and Denise Scott Brown, reprinted from *A View from the Campidoglio*, edited by Peter Arnell, Ted Bickford, and Catherine Bergart, (1984).

CONTENTS

Against Imitation

Plato

Of the many excellences which I perceive in the order of our State, there is none which upon reflection pleases me better than the rule about poetry.

To what do you refer?

To the rejection of imitative poetry, which certainly ought not to be received; as I see far more clearly now that the parts of the soul have been distinguished.

What do you mean?

Speaking in confidence, for I should not like to have my words repeated to the tragedians and the rest of the imitative tribe—but I do not mind saying to you, that all poetical imitations are ruinous to the understanding of the hearers, and that the knowledge of their true nature is the only antidote to them.

Explain the purport of your remark.

Well, I will tell you, although I have always from my earliest youth had an awe and love of Homer, which even now makes the words falter on my lips, for he is the great captain and teacher of the whole of that charming tragic company; but a man is not to be reverenced more than the truth, and therefore I will speak out.

Very good, he said.

Listen to me then, or rather, answer me.

Put your question.

Can you tell me what imitation is? for I really do not know.

A likely thing, then, that I should know.

Why not? for the duller eye may often see a thing sooner than the keener.

Very true, he said; but in your presence, even if I had any faint notion, I could not muster courage to utter it. Will you enquire yourself?

Well then, shall we begin the enquiry in our usual manner: Whenever a number of individuals have a common name, we assume them to have also a corresponding idea or form—do you understand me?

I do.

Let us take any common instance; there are beds and tables in the world—plenty of them, are there not?

Yes.

But there are only two ideas or forms of them—one the idea of a bed, the other of a table.

True.

An excerpt

And the maker of either of them makes a bed or he makes a table for our use, in accordance with the idea—that is our way of speaking in this and similar instances—but no artificer makes the ideas themselves: how could he?

Impossible.

And there is another artist—I should like to know what you would say of him.

Who is he?

One who is the maker of all the works of all other workmen.

What an extraordinary man!

Wait a little, and there will be more reason for your saying so. For this is he who is able to make not only vessels of every kind, but plants and animals, himself and all other things—the earth and heaven, and the things which are in heaven or under the earth; he makes the gods also.

He must be a wizard and no mistake.

Oh! you are incredulous, are you? Do you mean that there is no such maker or creator, or that in one sense there might be a maker of all these things but in another not? Do you see that there is a way in which you could make them all yourself?

What way?

An easy way enough; or rather, there are many ways in which the feat might be quickly and easily accomplished, none quicker than that of turning a mirror round and round—you would soon enough make the sun and the heavens, and the earth and yourself, and other animals and plants, and all the other things of which we were just now speaking, in the mirror.

Yes, he said; but they would be appearances only.

Very good, I said, you are coming to the point now. And the painter too is, as I conceive, just such another—a creator of appearances, is he not?

Of course.

But then I suppose you will say that what he creates is untrue. And yet there is a sense in which the painter also creates a bed?

Yes, he said, but not a real bed.

And what of the maker of the bed? were you not saying that he too makes, not the idea which, according to our view, is the essence of the bed, but only a particular bed?

Yes, I did.

Then if he does not make that which exists he cannot make true existence, but only some semblance of existence; and if any one were to say that the work of the maker of the bed, or of any other workman, has real existence, he could hardly be supposed to be speaking the truth.

At any rate, he replied, philosophers would say that he was not speaking the truth.

No wonder, then, that his work too is an indistinct expression of truth.

No wonder.

Suppose now that by the light of the examples just offered we enquire who this imitator is?

If you please.

Well then, here are three beds: one existing in nature, which is made by God, as I think that we may say—for no one else can be the maker?

No.

There is another which is the work of the carpenter?

Yes.

And the work of the painter is a third?

Yes.

Beds, then, are of three kinds, and there are three artists who superintend them: God, the maker of the bed, and the painter?

Yes, there are three of them.

God, whether from choice or from necessity, made one bed in nature and one only; two or more such ideal beds neither ever have been nor ever will be made by God.

Why is that?

Because even if He had made but two, a third would still appear behind them which both of them would have for their idea, and that would be the ideal bed and not the two others.

Very true, he said.

God knew this, and He desired to be the real maker of a real bed, not a particular maker of a particular bed, and therefore He created a bed which is essentially and by nature one only.

So we believe.

Shall we, then, speak of Him as the natural author or maker of the bed?

Yes, he replied; inasmuch as by the natural process of creation He is the author of this and of all other things.

And what shall we say of the carpenter—is not he also the maker of the bed?

Yes.

But would you call the painter a creator and maker?

Certainly not.

Yet if he is not the maker, what is he in relation to the bed?

I think, he said, that we may fairly designate him as the imitator of that which the others make.

Good, I said; then you call him who is third in the descent from nature an imitator?

Certainly, he said.

And the tragic poet is an imitator, and therefore, like all other imitators, he is thrice removed from the king and from the truth?

That appears to be so.

Then about the imitator we are agreed. And what about the painter?—I would like to know whether he may be thought to imitate that which originally exists in nature, or only the creations of artists?

The latter.

As they are or as they appear? you have still to determine this.

What do you mean?

I mean, that you may look at a bed from different points of view, obliquely or directly or from any other point of view, and the bed will appear different, but there is no difference in reality. And the same of all things.

Yes, he said, the difference is only apparent.

Now let me ask you another question: Which is the art of painting designed to be—an imitation of things as they are, or as they appear—of appearance or of reality?

Of appearance.

Then the imitator, I said, is a long way off the truth, and can do all things because he lightly touches on a small part of them, and that part an image. For example: A painter will paint a cobbler, carpenter, or any other artist, though he knows nothing of their arts; and, if he is a good artist, he may deceive children or simple persons, when he shows them his picture of a carpenter from a distance, and they will fancy that they are looking at a real carpenter.

Certainly.

And whenever any one informs us that he has found a man who knows all the arts, and all things else that anybody knows, and every single thing with a higher degree of accuracy than any other man—whoever tells us this, I think that we can only imagine him to be a simple creature who is likely to have been deceived by some wizard or actor whom he met, and whom he thought all-knowing, because he himself was unable to analyse the nature of knowledge and ignorance and imitation.

Most true.

And so, when we hear persons saying that the tragedians, and Homer, who is at their head, know all the arts and all things human, virtue as well as vice, and divine things too, for that the good poet cannot compose well unless he knows his subject, and that he who has not this knowledge can never be a poet, we ought to consider whether here also there may not be a similar illusion. Perhaps they may have come across imitators and been deceived by them; they may not have remembered when they saw their works that these were but imitations thrice removed from the truth, and could easily be made without any knowledge of the truth, because they are appearances only and not realities? Or, after all, they may be in the right, and poets do really know the things about which they seem to the many to speak so well?

The question, he said, should by all means be considered.

Now do you suppose that if a person were able to make the original as well as the image, he would seriously devote himself to the image-making branch? Would he allow imitation to be the ruling principle of his life, as if he had nothing higher in him?

I should say not.

The real artist, who knew what he was imitating, would be interested in realities and not in imitations; and would desire to leave as memorials of himself works many and fair; and, instead of being the author of encomiums, he would prefer to be the theme of them.

Yes, he said, that would be to him a source of much greater honour and profit.

Then, I said, we must put a question to Homer; not about medicine, or any of the arts to which his poems only incidentally refer: we are not going to ask him, or any other poet, whether he has cured patients like Asclepius, or left behind him a school of medicine such as the Asclepiads were, or whether he only talks about medicine and other arts at second-hand; but we have a right to know respecting military tactics, politics, education, which are the chiefest and noblest subjects of his poems, and we may fairly ask him about them. 'Friend Homer,' then we say to him, 'if you are only in the second remove from truth in what you say of virtue, and not in the third—not an image maker or imitator—and if you are able to discern what pursuits make men better or worse in private or public life, tell us what State was ever better governed by your help? The good order of Lacedaemon is due to Lycurgus, and many other cities great and small have been similarly benefited by others; but who says that you have been a good legislator to them and have done them any good? Italy and Sicily boast of Charondas, and there is Solon who is renowned among us; but what city has anything to say about you?' Is there any city which he might name?

I think not, said Glaucon; not even the Homerids themselves pretend that he was a legislator.

Well, but is there any war on record which was carried on successfully by him, or aided by his counsels, when he was alive?

There is not.

Or is there any invention of his, applicable to the arts or to human life, such as Thales the Milesian or Anacharsis the Scythian, and other ingenious men have conceived, which is attributed to him?

There is absolutely nothing of the kind. . . .

The Limits of Likeness

Ernst Gombrich

In his charming autobiography, the German illustrator Ludwig Richter relates how he and his friends, all young art students in Rome in the 1820s, visited the famous beauty spot of Tivoli and sat down to draw. They looked with surprise, but hardly with approval, at a group of French artists who approached the place with enormous baggage, carrying large quantities of paint which they applied to the canvas with big, coarse brushes. The Germans, perhaps roused by this self-confident artiness, were determined on the opposite approach. They selected the hardest, best-pointed pencils, which could render the motif firmly and minutely to its finest detail, and each bent down over his small piece of paper, trying to transcribe what he saw with the utmost fidelity. "We fell in love with every blade of grass, every tiny twig, and refused to let anything escape us. Every one tried to render the motif as objectively as possible."

Nevertheless, when they then compared the fruits of their efforts in the evening, their transcripts differed to a surprising extent. The mood, the color, even the outline

An excerpt

of the motif had undergone a subtle transformation in each of them. Richter goes on to describe how these different versions reflected the different dispositions of the four friends, for instance, how the melancholy painter had straightened the exuberant contours and emphasized the blue tinges. We might say he gives an illustration of the famous definition by Emile Zola, who called a work of art "a corner of nature seen through a temperament."

It is precisely because we are interested in this definition that we must probe it a little further. The "temperament" or "personality" of the artist, his selective preferences, may be one of the reasons for the transformation which the motif undergoes under the artist's hands, but there must be others—everything, in fact, which we bundle together into the word "style," the style of the period and the style of the artist. . . .

The very point of Richter's story, after all, is that style rules even where the artist wishes to reproduce nature faithfully, and trying to analyze these limits to objectivity may help us get nearer to the riddle of style. One of these limits we know from the last chapter; it is indicated in Richter's story by the contrast between coarse brush and fine pencil. The artist, clearly, can render only what his tool and his medium are capable of rendering. His technique restricts his freedom of choice. The features and relationships the pencil picks out will differ from those the brush can indicate. Sitting in front of his motif, pencil in hand, the artist will, therefore, look out for those aspects which can be rendered in lines—as we say in a pardonable abbreviation, he will tend to see his motif in terms of lines, while, brush in hand, he sees it in terms of masses.

The question of why style should impose similar limitations is less easily answered, least of all when we do not know whether the artist's intentions were the same as those of Richter and his friends.

Historians of art have explored the regions where Cézanne and van Gogh set up their easels and have photographed their motifs. Such comparisons will always retain their fascination since they almost allow us to look over the artist's shoulder—and who does not wish he had this privilege? But however instructive such confrontations may be when handled with care, we must clearly beware of the fallacy of "stylization." Should we believe the photograph represents the "objective truth" while the painting records the artist's subjective vision—the way he transformed "what he saw"? Can we here compare "the image on the retina" with the "image in the mind"? Such speculations easily lead into a morass of unprovables. Take the image on the artist's retina. It sounds scientific enough, but actually there never was *one* such image which we could single out for comparison with either photograph or painting. What there was was an endless succession of innumerable images as the painter scanned the landscape in front of him, and these images sent a complex pattern of impulses through the optic nerves to his brain. Even the artist knew nothing of these events, and we know even less. How far the picture that formed in his mind corresponded to or deviated from the photograph it is even less profitable to ask. What we do know is that these artists went out into nature to look for material for a picture and their artistic wisdom led them to organize the elements of the landscape into works of art of marvelous complexity that bear as much relationship to a surveyor's record as a poem bears to a police report.

Does this mean, then, that we are altogether on a useless quest? That artistic truth differs so much from prosaic truth that the question of objectivity must never be asked? I do not think so. We must only be a little more circumspect in our formulation of the question. . . .

Now the historian knows that the information pictures were expected to provide differed widely in different periods. Not only were images scarce in the past, but so were the public's opportunities to check their captions. How many people ever saw their ruler in the flesh at sufficiently close quarters to recognize his likeness? How many traveled widely enough to tell one city from another? It is hardly surprising, therefore, that pictures of people and places changed their captions with sovereign disregard for truth. The print sold on the market as a portrait of a king would be altered to represent his successor or enemy.

There is a famous example of this indifference to truthful captions in one of the most ambitious publishing projects of the early printing press, Hartmann Schedel's so-called "Nuremberg Chronicle" with woodcuts by Dürer's teacher Wolgemut. What an opportunity such a volume should give the historian to see what the world was like at the time of Columbus! But as we turn the pages of this big folio, we find the same woodcut of a medieval city recurring with different captions as Damascus, Ferrara, Milan, and Mantua. Unless we are prepared to believe these cities were as indistinguishable from one another as their suburbs may be today, we must conclude that neither the publisher nor the public minded whether the captions told the truth. All they were expected to do was to bring home to the reader that these names stood for cities. . . .

In our culture, where pictures exist in such profusion, it is difficult to demonstrate this basic fact. There are freshmen in art schools who have facility in the objective rendering of motifs that would appear to belie this assumption. But those who have given art classes in other cultural settings tell a different story. James Cheng, who taught painting to a group of Chinese trained in different conventions, once told me of a sketching expedition he made with his students to a famous beauty spot, one of Peking's old city gates. The task baffled them. In the end, one of the students asked to be given at least a picture post card of the building so that they would have something to copy. It is stories such as these, stories of breakdowns, that explain why art has a history and artists need a style adapted to a task.

I cannot illustrate this revealing incident. But luck allows us to study the next stage, as it were—the adjustment of the traditional vocabulary of Chinese art to the unfamiliar task of topographical portrayal in the Western sense. For some decades Chiang Yee, a Chinese writer and painter of great gifts and charm, has delighted us with contemplative records of the Silent Traveller, books in which he tells of his encounters with scenes and people of the English and Irish countryside and elsewhere. I take an illustration from the volume on the English Lakeland.

It is a view of Derwentwater. Here we have crossed the line that separates documentation from art. Mr. Chiang Yee certainly enjoys the adaptation of the Chinese idiom to a new purpose; he wants us to see the English scenery for once "through Chinese eyes." But it is precisely for this reason that it is so instructive to compare his view with a typical "picturesque" rendering from the Romantic period. We see how the relatively rigid vocabulary of the Chinese tradition acts as a selective screen which admits only the features for which schemata exist. The artist will be attracted by motifs which can be rendered in his idiom. As he scans the landscape, the sights which can be matched successfully with the schemata he has learned to handle will leap forward as centers of attention. The style, like the medium, creates a mental set which makes the artist look for certain aspects in the scene around him that he can render. Painting is an activity, and the artist will therefore tend to see what he paints rather than to paint what he sees.

It is this interaction between style and preference which Nietzsche summed up in his mordant comment on the claims of realism:

"All Nature faithfully"—But by what feint
Can Nature be subdued to art's constraint?
Her smallest fragment is still infinite!
And so he paints but what he likes in it.
What does he like? He likes, what he can paint!

There is more in this observation than just a cool reminder of the limitations of artistic means. We catch a glimpse of the reasons why these limitations will never obtrude themselves within the domain of art itself. Art presupposes mastery, and the greater the artist the more surely will he instinctively avoid a task where his mastery would fail to serve him. The layman may wonder whether Giotto could have painted a view of Fiesole in sunshine, but the historian will suspect that, lacking the means, he would not have wanted to, or rather that he could not have wanted to. We like to assume, somehow, that where there is a will there is also a way, but in matters of art the maxim should read that only where there is a way is there also a will. The individual can enrich the ways and means that his culture offers him; he can hardly wish for something that he has never known is possible. . . .

Need we infer from this fact that there is no such thing as an objective likeness? That it makes no sense to ask, for instance, whether Chiang Yee's view of Derwentwater is more or less correct than the nineteenth-century lithograph in which the formulas of classical landscapes were applied to the same task? It is a tempting conclusion and one which recommends itself to the teacher of art appreciation because it brings home to the layman how much of what we call "seeing" is conditioned by habits and expectations. It is all the more important to clarify how far this relativism will take us. . . .

From the point of view of information there is surely no difficulty in discussing portrayal. To say of a drawing that it is a correct view of Tivoli does not mean, of course, that Tivoli is bounded by wiry lines. It means that those who understand the notation will derive *no false information* from the drawing—whether it gives the contour in a few lines or picks out "every blade of grass" as Richter's friends wanted to do. The complete portrayal might be the one which gives as much correct information about the spot as we would obtain if we looked at it from the very spot where the artist stood.

Styles, like languages, differ in the sequence of articulation and in the number of questions they allow the artist to ask; and so complex is the information that reaches us from the visible world that no picture will ever embody it all. This is not due to the subjectivity of vision but to its richness. Where the artist has to copy a human product he can, of course, produce a facsimile which is indistinguishable from the original. The forger of bank-notes succeeds only too well in effacing his personality and the limitations of a period style.

But what matters to us is that the correct portrait, like the useful map, is an end product on a long road through schema and correction. It is not a faithful record of a visual experience but the faithful construction of a relational model.

Neither the subjectivity of vision nor the sway of conventions need lead us to deny that such a model can be constructed to any required degree of accuracy. What is decisive here is clearly the word "required." The form of a representation cannot be divorced from its purpose and the requirements of the society in which the given visual language gains currency.

Reality Remade

Nelson Goodman

Realism is relative, determined by the system of representation standard for a given culture or person at a given time. Newer or older or alien systems are accounted artificial or unskilled. For a Fifth-Dynasty Egyptian the straightforward way of representing something is not the same as for an eighteenth-century Japanese; and neither way is the same as for an early twentieth-century Englishman. Each would to some extent have to learn how to read a picture in either of the other styles. This relativity is obscured by our tendency to omit specifying a frame of reference when it is our own. "Realism" thus often comes to be used as the name for a particular style or system of representation. Just as on this planet we usually think of objects as fixed if they are at a constant position in relation to the earth, so in this period and place we usually think of paintings as literal or realistic if they are in a traditional European style of representation. But such egocentric ellipsis must not tempt us to infer that these objects (or any others) are absolutely fixed, or that such pictures (or any others) are absolutely realistic.

An excerpt
Footnotes have been renumbered.—Ed.

Shifts in standard can occur rather rapidly. The very effectiveness that may attend judicious departure from a traditional system of representation sometimes inclines us at least temporarily to install the newer mode as standard. We then speak of an artist's having achieved a new degree of realism, or having found new means for the realistic rendering of (say) light or motion. What happens here is something like the 'discovery' that not the earth but the sun is 'really fixed.' Advantages of a new frame of reference, partly because of their novelty, encourage its enthronement on some occasions in place of the customary frame. Nevertheless, whether an object is 'really fixed' or a picture is realistic depends at any time entirely upon what frame or mode is then standard. Realism is a matter not of any constant or absolute relationship between a picture and its object but of a relationship between the system of representation employed in the picture and the standard system. Most of the time, of course, the traditional system is taken as standard; and the literal or realistic or naturalistic system of representation is simply the customary one.

Realistic representation, in brief, depends not upon imitation or illusion or information but upon inculcation. Almost any picture may represent almost anything; that is, given picture and object there is usually a system of representation, a plan of correlation, under which the picture represents the object.[1] How correct the picture is under that system depends upon how accurate is the information about the object that is obtained by reading the picture according to that system. But how literal or realistic the picture is depends upon how standard the system is. If representation is a matter of choice and correctness a matter of information, realism is a matter of habit.

Our addiction, in the face of overwhelming counterevidence, to thinking of resemblance as the measure of realism is easily understood in these terms. Representational customs, which govern realism, also tend to generate resemblance. That a picture looks like nature often means only that it looks the way nature is usually painted. Again, what will deceive me into supposing that an object of a given kind is before me depends upon what I have noticed about such objects, and this in turn is affected by the way I am used to seeing them depicted. Resemblance and deceptiveness, far from being constant and independent sources and criteria of representational practice, are in some degree products of it. . . . [2]

---

[1]Indeed, there are usually many such systems. A picture that under one (unfamiliar) system is a correct but highly unrealistic representation of an object may under another (the standard) system be a realistic but very incorrect representation of the same object. Only if accurate information is yielded under the standard system will the picture represent the object both correctly and literally.

[2]Neither here nor elsewhere have I argued that there is no constant relation of resemblance; judgments of similarity in selected and familiar respects are, even though rough and fallible, as objective and categorical as any that are made in describing the world. But judgments of complex overall resemblance are another matter. In the first place, they depend upon the aspects or factors in terms of which the objects in question are compared; and this depends heavily on conceptual and perceptual habit. In the second place, even with these factors determined, similarities along the several axes are not immediately commensurate,

Let us speak of a work of art as *autographic* if and only if the distinction between original and forgery of it is significant; or better, if and only if even the most exact duplication of it does not thereby count as genuine. If a work of art is autographic, we may also call that art autographic. Thus painting is autographic, music nonautographic, or *allographic*. These terms are introduced purely for convenience; nothing is implied concerning the relative individuality of expression demanded by or attainable in these arts. Now the problem before us is to account for the fact that some arts but not others are autographic.

The Work of Art in the Age of Mechanical Reproduction

Walter Benjamin

In principle a work of art has always been reproducible. Man-made artifacts could always be imitated by men. Replicas were made by pupils in practice of their craft, by masters for diffusing their works, and, finally, by third parties in the pursuit of gain. Mechanical reproduction of a work of art, however, represents something new. Historically, it advanced intermittently and in leaps at long intervals, but with accelerated intensity. The Greeks knew only two procedures of technically reproducing works of art: founding and stamping. Bronzes, terra cottas, and coins were the only art works which they could produce in quantity. All others were unique and could not be mechanically reproduced. With the woodcut graphic art became mechanically reproducible for the first time, long before script became reproducible by print. The enormous changes which printing, the mechanical reproduction of writing, has brought about in literature are a familiar story. However, within the phenomenon which we are examining from the perspective of world history, print is merely a special, though par-

---

and the degree of total resemblance will depend upon how the several factors are weighted. Normally, for example, nearness in geographical location has little to do with our judgment of resemblance among buildings but much to do with our judgment of resemblance among building lots. The assessment of total resemblance is subject to influences galore, and our representational customs are not least among these. In sum, I have sought to show that insofar as resemblance is a constant and objective relation, resemblance between a picture and what is represents does not coincide with realism; and that insofar as resemblance does coincide with realism, the criteria of resemblance vary with changes in representational practice.

ticularly important, case. During the Middle Ages engraving and etching were added to the woodcut; at the beginning of the nineteenth century lithography made its appearance.

With lithography the technique of reproduction reached an essentially new stage. This much more direct process was distinguished by the tracing of the design on a stone rather than its incision on a block of wood or its etching on a copperplate and permitted graphic art for the first time to put its products on the market, not only in large numbers as hitherto, but also in daily changing forms. Lithography enabled graphic art to illustrate everyday life, and it began to keep pace with printing. But only a few decades after its invention, lithography was surpassed by photography. For the first time in the process of pictorial reproduction, photography freed the hand of the most important artistic functions which henceforth devolved only upon the eye looking into a lens. Since the eye perceives more swiftly than the hand can draw, the process of pictorial reproduction was accelerated so enormously that it could keep pace with speech. A film operator shooting a scene in the studio captures the images at the speed of an actor's speech. Just as lithography virtually implied the illustrated newspaper, so did photography foreshadow the sound film. The technical reproduction of sound was tackled at the end of the last century. These convergent endeavors made predictable a situation which Paul Valéry pointed up in this sentence: "Just as water, gas, and electricity are brought into our houses from far off to satisfy our needs in response to a minimal effort, so we shall be supplied with visual or auditory images, which will appear and disappear at a simple movement of the hand, hardly more than a sign." Around 1900 technical reproduction had reached a standard that not only permitted it to reproduce all transmitted works of art and thus to cause the most profound change in their impact upon the public; it also had captured a place of its own among the artistic processes. For the study of this standard nothing is more revealing than the nature of the repercussions that these two different manifestations—the reproduction of works of art and the art of the film—have had on art in its traditional form.

Even the most perfect reproduction of a work of art is lacking in one element: its presence in time and space, its unique existence at the place where it happens to be. This unique existence of the work of art determined the history to which it was subject throughout the time of its existence. This includes the changes which it may have suffered in physical condition over the years as well as the various changes in its ownership. The traces of the first can be revealed only by chemical or physical analyses which it is impossible to perform on a reproduction; changes of ownership are subject to a tradition which must be traced from the situation of the original.

The presence of the original is the prerequisite to the concept of authenticity. Chemical analyses of the patina of a bronze can help to establish this, as does the proof that a given manuscript of the Middle Ages stems from an archive of the fifteenth century. The whole sphere of authenticity is outside technical—and, of course, not only technical—reproducibility. Confronted with its manual reproduction, which was usually branded as a forgery, the original preserved all its authority; not so *vis à vis* technical reproduction. The reason is twofold. First, process reproduction is more independent of the original than manual reproduction. For example, in photography, process reproduction can bring out those aspects of the original that are unattainable to the naked eye yet accessible to the lens, which is adjustable and chooses its angle at will. And photographic reproduction, with the aid of certain processes, such as enlargement or slow motion, can capture images which escape natural vision. Secondly, technical reproduction can put the copy of the original into situations which would be out of reach for the original itself. Above all, it enables the original to meet the beholder halfway, be it in the form of a photograph or a phonograph record. The cathedral leaves its locale to be received in the studio of a lover of art; the choral production, performed in an auditorium or in the open air, resounds in the drawing room.

The situations into which the product of mechanical reproduction can be brought may not touch the actual work of art, yet the quality of its presence is always depreciated. This holds not only for the art work but also, for instance, for a landscape which passes in review before the spectator in a movie. In the case of the art object, a most sensitive nucleus—namely, its authenticity—is interfered with whereas no natural object is vulnerable on that score. The authenticity of a thing is the essence of all that is transmissible from its beginning, ranging from its substantive duration to its testimony to the history which it has experienced. Since the historical testimony rests on the authenticity, the former, too, is jeopardized by reproduction when substantive duration ceases to matter. And what is really jeopardized when the historical testimony is affected is the authority of the object.

One might subsume the eliminated element in the term "aura" and go on to say: *that which withers in the age of mechanical reproduction is the aura of the work of art.* This is a symptomatic process whose significance points beyond the realm of art. One might generalize by saying: the technique of reproduction detaches the reproduced object from the domain of tradition. By making many reproductions it substitutes a plurality of copies for a unique existence. And in permitting the reproduction to meet the beholder or listener in his own particular situation, it reactivates the object reproduced. These two processes lead to a tremendous shattering of tradition which is the obverse of the contemporary crisis and renewal of mankind. Both processes are intimately connected with the contemporary mass movements. Their most powerful agent is the film. Its social significance, particularly in its most positive form, is inconceivable without its destructive, cathartic aspect, that is, the liquidation of the traditional value of the cultural heritage. This phenomenon is most palpable in the great historical films. It extends to ever new positions. In 1927 Abel Gance exclaimed enthusiastically: "Shakespeare, Rembrandt, Beethoven will make films . . . all legends, all mythologies and all myths, all founders of religion, and the very religions . . . await their exposed resurrection, and the heroes crowd each other at the gate." Presumably without intending it, he issued an invitation to a far-reaching liquidation.

During long periods of history, the mode of human sense perception changes with humanity's entire mode of existence. The manner in which human sense perception is organized, the medium in which it is accomplished, is determined not only by nature but by historical circumstances as well. The fifth century, with its great shifts of population, saw the birth of the late Roman art industry and the Vienna Genesis, and there developed not only an art different from that of antiquity but also a new kind of perception. The scholars of the Viennese school, Riegl and Wickhoff, who resisted the weight of classical tradition under which these later art forms has been buried, were the first to draw conclusions from them concerning the organization of perception at the time. However far-reaching their insight, these scholars limited themselves to showing the significant, formal hallmark which characterized perception in late Roman times. They did not attempt—and, perhaps, saw no way—to show the social transformations expressed by these changes of perception. The conditions for an analogous insight are more favorable in the present. And if changes in the medium of contemporary perception can be comprehended as decay of the aura, it is possible to show its social causes.

The concept of aura which was proposed above with reference to historical objects may usefully be illustrated with reference to the aura of natural ones. We define the aura of the latter as the unique phenomenon of a distance, however close it may be. If, while resting on a summer afternoon, you follow with your eyes a mountain range on the horizon or a branch which casts its shadow over you, you experience the aura of those mountains, of that branch. This image makes it easy to comprehend the social bases of the contemporary decay of the aura. It rests on two circumstances, both of which are related to the increasing significance of the masses in contemporary life. Namely, the desire of contemporary masses to bring things "closer" spatially and humanly, which is just as ardent as their bent toward overcoming the uniqueness of every reality by accepting its reproduction. Every day the urge grows stronger to get hold of an object at very close range by way of its likeness, its reproduction. Unmistakably, reproduction as offered by picture magazines and newsreels differs from the image seen by the unarmed eye. Uniqueness and permanence are as closely linked in the latter as are transitoriness and reproducibility in the former. To pry an object from its shell, to destroy its aura, is the mark of a perception whose "sense of the universal equality of things" has increased to such a degree that it extracts it even from a unique object by means of reproduction. Thus is manifested in the field of perception what in the theoretical sphere is noticeable in the increasing importance of statistics. The adjustment of reality to the masses and of the masses to reality is a process of unlimited scope, as much for thinking as for perception.

The uniqueness of a work of art is inseparable from its being imbedded in the fabric of tradition. This tradition itself is thoroughly alive and extremely changeable. An ancient statue of Venus, for example, stood in a different traditional context with the Greeks, who made it an object of veneration, than with the clerics of the Middle Ages, who viewed it as an ominous idol. Both of them, however, were equally confronted with its uniqueness, that is, its aura. Originally the contextual integration of art in tradition found its expression in the cult. We know that the earliest art works originated in the service of a ritual—first the magical, then the religious kind. It is significant that the existence of the work of art with reference to its aura is never entirely separated from its ritual function. In other words, the unique value of the "authentic" work of art has its basis in ritual, the location of its original use value. This ritualistic basis, however remote, is still recognizable as secularized ritual even in the most profane forms of the cult of beauty. The secular cult of beauty, developed during the Renaissance and prevailing for three centuries, clearly showed that ritualistic basis in its decline and the first deep crisis which befell it. With the advent of the first truly revolutionary means of reproduction, photography, simultaneously with the rise of socialism, art sensed the approaching crisis which has become evident a century later. At the time, art reacted with the doctrine of *l'art pour l'art,* that is, with a theology of art. This gave rise to what might be called a negative theology in the form of the idea of "pure" art, which not only denied any social function of art but also any categorizing by subject matter. (In poetry, Mallarmé was the first to take this position.)

An analysis of art in the age of mechanical reproduction must do justice to these relationships, for they lead us to an all-important insight: for the fist time in world history, mechanical reproduction emancipates the work of art from its parasitical dependence on ritual. To an ever greater degree the work of art reproduced becomes the work of art designed for reproducibility. From a photographic negative, for example, one can make any number of prints; to ask for the "authentic" print makes no sense. But the instant the criterion of authenticity ceases to be applicable to artistic production, the total function of art is reversed. Instead of being based on ritual, it begins to be based on another practice—politics. . . .

Why Photography Is Not Art

Roger Scruton

The ideal painting stands in a certain 'intentional' relation to a subject. In other words, if a painting represents a subject, it does not follow that the subject exists nor, if it does exist, that the painting represents the subject as it is. Moreover, if x is a painting of a man, it does not follow that there is some *particular* man of which x is the painting. Furthermore, the painting stands in this intentional relation to its subject because of a representational act, the artist's act, and in characterizing the relation between a painting and its subject we are also describing the artist's intention. The successful realization of that intention lies in the creation of an appearance, an appearance which in some way leads the spectator to recognize the subject.

The ideal photograph also stands in a certain relation to a subject: a photograph is a photograph *of* something. But the relation is here causal and not intentional. In other words, if a photograph is a photograph of a subject, it follows that the subject

---

An excerpt

exists, and if *x* is the photograph of a man, there is a particular man of whom *x* is the photograph. It also follows, though for different reasons, that the subject is, roughly, as it appears in the photograph. In characterizing the relation between the ideal photograph and its subject, one is characterizing not an intention but a causal process, and while there is, as a rule, an intentional act involved, this is not an essential part of the photographic relation. The ideal photograph also yields an appearance, but the appearance is not interesting as the realization of an intention but rather as a record of how an actual object looked. . . .

Although there is not space to discuss fully the concept of 'understanding' that is involved here, it is worth mentioning the following point: to understand a painting involves understanding thoughts. These thoughts are, in a sense, communicated by the painting. They underlie the painter's intention, and at the same time they inform our way of seeing the canvas. Such thoughts determine the perception of the man who sees with understanding, and it is at least partly in terms of our apprehension of thoughts that we must describe what we see in the picture. We see not only a man on a horse but a man of a certain character and bearing. And *what* we see is determined not by independent properties of the subject but by our understanding of the painting. It is the way the eyes are painted that gives that sense of authority, the particular lie of the arm that reveals the arrogant character, and so on. In other words, properties of the medium influence not only what is seen in the picture but also the way it is seen. Moreover, they present to us a vision that we attribute not to ourselves but to another man; we think of ourselves as sharing in the vision of the artist, and the omnipresence of intention changes our experience from something private into something shared. The picture presents us not merely with the perception of a man but with a thought about him, a thought embodied in a perceptual form. . . .

Now, *one* difference between an aesthetic interest in a picture, and an interest in the picture as a surrogate for its subject, lies in the kind of reason that might be given for the interest. (And to give the reasons for an interest is to give an account of its intentional object and therefore of the interest itself.) If I ask a man why he is looking at a picture, there are several kinds of reply that he might give. In one case his reasons will be reasons for an interest only in the things depicted: they will describe properties of the subject which make it interesting. Here the interest in the picture is derivative: it lies in the fact that the picture reveals properties of its subject. The picture is being treated as a means of access to the subject, and it is therefore dispensable to the extent that there is a better means to hand (say, the subject itself). With that case one may contrast two others. First, there is the case where the man's reasons refer only to properties of the picture—to pictorial properties, such as colour, shape, and line—and do not mention the subject. For such a man the picture has interest as an abstract composition, and its representational nature is wholly irrelevant to him. Second, there is the case where the reasons for the interest are reasons for an interest in the *picture* (in the way it looks) even though they make essential reference to the subject and can be understood as reasons only by someone who understands the reference to the subject. For example, the observer may refer to a particular gesture of a certain figure, and a particular way of painting that gesture, as revelatory of the subject's character (for example, the barmaid's hands on the counter in Manet's *Bar aux Folies-Bergère*). Clearly, that is a reason not only for an interest in the subject but also (and primarily) for an interest in the picture, since it gives a reason for an interest in something which can be understood only by looking at the picture. Such an interest leads naturally to another, to an interest in the use of the medium—in the way the painting presents its subject and therefore in the way in which the subject is seen by the painter. Here it could not be said that the painting is being treated as a surrogate for its subject: it is *itself* the object of interest and irreplaceable by the thing depicted. The interest is not in representation for the sake of its subject but in representation for its own sake. And it is such an interest that forms the core of the aesthetic experience of pictorial art, and which—if analysed more fully—would explain not only the value of that experience but also the nature and value of the art which is its object. We see at once that such an interest is not, and cannot be, an interest in the literal truth of the picture. . . .

One of the most important differences between photography and portraiture as traditionally practised lies in the relation of each to time. It is characteristic of photography that, being understood in terms of a causal relation to its subject, it is thought of as revealing something momentary about its subject—how the subject looked at a particular moment. And that sense of the moment is seldom lost in photography, for reasons that will shortly be apparent. Portrait painting, however, aims to capture the sense of time and to represent its subject as extended in time, even in the process of displaying a particular moment of its existence. Portraiture is not an art of the momentary, and its aim is not merely to capture fleeting appearances. The aim of painting is to give insight, and the creation of an appearance is important mainly as the expression of thought. While a causal relation is a relation between events, there is no such narrow restriction on the subject-matter of a thought . . .

With an ideal photograph it is neither necessary nor even possible that the photographer's intention should enter as a serious factor in determining how the picture is seen. It is recognized at once for what it is—not as an interpretation of reality but as a presentation of how something looked. In some sense, looking at a photograph is a substitute for looking at the thing itself. Consider for example, the most 'realistic' of all photographic media, the television. It seems scarcely more contentious to say that I saw someone on the television—that is, that in watching the television I saw *him*—than to say that I saw him in a mirror. Television is like a mirror: it does not so much destroy as embellish that elaborate causal chain which is the natural process of visual perception. . . .

It follows, first, that the subject of the ideal photograph must exist; secondly, that it must appear roughly as it appears in the photograph; and thirdly, that its appearance in the photograph is its appearance at a particular moment of its existence.

The first of those features is an immediate consequence of the fact that the relation between a photograph and its subject is a causal relation. If *a* is the cause of *b*, then the existence of *b* is sufficient for the existence of *a*. The photograph lacks that quality of 'intentional inexistence' which is characteristic of painting. The ideal photograph, therefore, is incapable of representing anything unreal; if a photograph is a photograph of a man, then there is some particular man of whom it is a photograph.

Of course I may take a photograph of a draped nude and call it *Venus,* but insofar as this can be understood as an exercise in fiction, it should not be thought of as a photographic representation of Venus but rather as the photograph of a representation of Venus. In other words, the process of fictional representation occurs not in the photograph but in the subject: it is the *subject* which represents Venus; the photograph does no more than disseminate its visual character to other eyes. This is not to say that the model is (unknown to herself) acting Venus. It is not she who is representing Venus but the photographer, who uses her in his representation. But the representational act, the act which embodies the representational thought, is completed before the photograph is ever taken. As we shall see, this fictional incompetence of photography is of great importance in our understanding of the cinema; but it also severely limits the aesthetic significance of 'representation' in photography. As we saw earlier, representation in art has a special significance precisely because of the possibility that we can understand it—in the sense of understanding its content—while being indifferent to, or unconcerned with, its literal truth. That is why fictional representation is not merely an important form of representational art but in fact the primary form of it, the form through which the aesthetic understanding finds its principal mode of expression.

One may wish to argue that my example is a special one, that there are other ways of creating fictional representation which are essentially photographic. In other words, it is not necessary for the photographer to create an independent representation in order for his photograph to be fictional. Suppose he were to take a photograph of a drunken tramp and label it *Silenus.* Would that not be a fictional photograph, comparable, indeed, to a painting of Silenus in which a drunken tramp was used as a model? . . .

The camera, then, is being used not to represent something but to point to it. The subject, once located, plays its own special part in an independent process of representation. The camera is not essential to that process: a gesturing finger would have served just as well. If the example shows that photographs can be representations, then it shows the same of fingers. To accept that conclusion is to fail to distinguish between what is accidental and what is essential in the expression of a representational thought. It is to open the way toward the theory that everything which plays a part in the expression of thought is itself a representation. Such a view does not account for the aesthetic significance of representations. It also, however, and far more seriously, implies that there is no distinction between representational and nonrepresentational art. The concept of representation that I am assuming makes such a distinction, and it makes it for very good reasons. I am not tempted by such dubious examples to abandon it. One might put the point by saying that a painting, like a sentence, is a *complete* expression of the thought which it contains. Painting is a sufficient vehicle of representational thought, and there may be no better way of expressing what a painting says. That is why representation can be thought of as an intrinsic property of a painting and not just as a property of some process of which the painting forms a part. . . .

Let us assume, however, that the photographer could intentionally exert over his image just the kind of control that is exercised in the other representational arts. The question is, How far can this control be extended? Certainly there will be an infinite number of things that lie outside his control. Dust on a sleeve, freckles on a face, wrinkles on a hand: such minutiae will always depend initially upon the prior situation of the subject. When the photographer sees the photographic plate, he may still wish to assert his control, choosing just this colour here, just that number of wrinkles or that texture of skin. He can proceed to paint things out or in, to touch up, alter, or *pasticher* as he pleases. But of course he has now become a painter, precisely through taking representation seriously. The photograph has been reduced to a kind of frame around which he paints, a frame that imposes upon him largely unnecessary constraints. . . .

Photography is not representation; nor is it representation when used in the cinema. A film is a photograph of a dramatic representation, and whatever representational properties belong to it belong by virtue of the representation that is effected in the dramatic action, that is, by virtue of the words and activities of the actors in the film. *Ivan the Terrible* represents the life of Ivan, not because the camera was directed at *him,* but because it was directed at an actor who *played the part of* Ivan. Certainly the camera has its role in presenting the action, much as the apparatus of production has its role on the stage. It directs the audience's attention to this or that feature and creates, too, its own peculiar effects of atmosphere. Proper use of the camera may create an interest in situations that could not be portrayed on the stage. Hence photography permits the extension of dramatic representation into areas where previously it would not have been possible, just as music, which is not a representational art, enabled Wagner to create for the first time a theatrical representation of a cosmic theme. (Consider, for example, the camera in Bergman's *Persona,* where it is used to create a dramatic situation between two characters, one of whom never speaks. Such mastery is perhaps rare, but is has existed as an ideal since the earliest days of cinema.) Nonetheless, the process of photography does not, because it cannot, *create* the representation. Thus documentary films are in no sense representations of their subject-matter. (Which is not to say that they cannot involve the realization of elaborate aesthetic ideas: it is hardly necessary to mention Leni Riefenstahl's film of the Berlin Olympics.) A cinematic record of an occurrence is not a representation of it, any more than a recording of a concert is a representation of its sound. As all must agree, representation in the cinema involves an *action,* in just the way that a play involves an action. The action is understood when the audience realizes that the figure photographed is attempting to portray adventures, actions, and feelings which are not his own, and yet which are nevertheless the proper subject-matter of aesthetic interest. It follows that the fundamental constraints which the cinema must obey as an art form—those constraints which are integral to its very nature as a representational art—are dramatic ones, involving the representation of character and action. ('Dramatic' here does not mean 'theatrical,' but is applied in the sense which Henry James gave to it when he spoke of the novel as a form of dramatic art.) To succeed as cinema, a film must have true characters, and it must be true to them; the director can no more sentimentalize with impunity than can the novelist or the playwright. The true source of the badness of most cinema lies, of course, in the fact that the gorgeous irrelevancies of photography obscure the sentimentality of the dramatic aim. . . .

What's Special About Photography?

Ted Cohen

The single most pervasive conviction about photographs is that they stand in some peculiar relation to the world, a relation not shared by other pictures. We might try to put this by saying that a photograph must be *of* something. That is not clear enough, however, even for getting started, because it is ambiguous. If 'being a photograph of' means being a picture of, and any picture of *I* guarantees the existence of *I,* then the statement that every photograph must be of something is false. On the other hand, if 'being a photograph of' means being a causal sequel to something's reflection or emission of light, then the statement that every photograph must be of something is true—but this is an odd sense of 'photograph of' which is not congruent with the normal sense of 'picture of' or of 'photograph of.' A photograph certainly guarantees the existence of a light source, but that much follows trivially from the meaning of the word 'photograph.'

The conviction that photographs hold a special relation to the world seems most often to amount to the idea that a photograph is a *fossil.* Perhaps this idea is defensible, but fossils are not, in general, pictures. The amplified idea, perhaps, is that a photograph is a picture of whatever it is a fossil of. I would not like to defend this formulation, because of cases like this:

> You have a family photograph showing several people on the beach. In the upper right there is dark speck. As a matter of fact, although no one could determine this by looking at the photograph, that speck is there because Uncle Fritz was frolicking in the waves far off shore at the instant the shutter snapped (and, as another matter of fact, the photographer didn't even notice him).

Do you think this photograph is a *picture* of Uncle Fritz? I am not sure, and I'm not entirely comfortable even with the assertion that it is, or contains, a *photograph* of him. What makes me uncomfortable is the knowledge that this photograph might look exactly the same if Uncle Fritz had been out to lunch but a piece of dirt had been on the camera lens or if a speck of lint had been on the enlarger's lens or if a stray shaft of light had struck the undeveloped photographic paper. And yet in the photograph as we are imagining it, there is no doubt that the speck is a fossil of Fritz; as a matter of relatively simple causation, it is there in the photograph because Uncle Fritz was there in the waves.

We need a better idea than that a photograph is a picture of whatever it is a fossil of. A promising idea is that it is a fossil of whatever it happens to be a picture of. There

---

An excerpt

is no doubt that the speck is a fossil of Fritz. Whether it is a photograph of him now depends upon whether it is a picture of him, and that is a question to be decided independently, and in any case this example and ones like it cease to be troublesome. It is an idea like this, I believe, which has led Kendall Walton to assert that photographs are "transparent," by which he means that in them we see—literally—what they depict. In a photograph of Ken you see Ken. I see less in this idea than Walton does but I am not sure that he is wrong. . . .

Perhaps a photograph is like a natural child, while other pictures are like adopted children. An adopted child may resemble a parent, and to some extent this may be due to its acquisition of mannerisms, posture, etc. which do come from the adoptive parents. And a natural child may not resemble the parent, or it may resemble it only with regard to this set of acquired, environmental features. But if it does resemble the parent, then we think that the resemblance is the result of genetic influence—a kind of basic, direct causation. So with photographs. A photograph may not resemble its subject, and a non-photographic picture may resemble its subject; but when a photograph does resemble its subject we think that the resemblance is the result of some basic, direct causation.

We look for parents in their children. We look for subjects in their photographs. If we find parents in their adopted children, or subjects in non-photographic pictures, we attribute this to artifice. If we find them in natural children or photographs, we attribute this to nature. I do not doubt that we do this. I wonder whether we are sensible to do it. Some cases, and they are not atypical, are mixed and complex. When I was a child, people remarked that I looked like my father when seen walking down the street, and the same thing has been said about my son and me. The noted similarity has many components. There are size, shape of body, relative length of limbs, for instance, but there are also posture and manner of walking. This manner incorporates speed, gait, placement of heel and toe, and motion of arms, while the posture includes the angle of head and torso. Some of these characteristics would be shared by my son, probably, if he were adopted and had spent as many years walking with me, but some would not. And some would be partial. For instance if my son's neck and torso were larger—if, say, I had adopted the child of a football player, a defensive lineman—then he would likely acquire a semblance of my walking posture but not a complete one. As things stand, some of my son's walking similarity seems due to genetics and some to habits acquired in his association with me. To these two constituents, the first apparently more directly and simply natural than the other, although the other is not "unnatural," might have been added characteristics developed in him by my explicit artifice. I might, for instance, have ordered him to walk in a certain way or suggested that he assume an erect posture. In the end, if you say that he looks like me, you will not have an easy time analyzing the similarity into discrete, simple parts, some natural and some not.

You will not have a much easier time explaining the resemblance of a photograph to its subject. The fact that the photograph shows a man with close-set, brooding eyes may be due to the fact that the subject has such eyes, but it may also be due to the angle from which the photographer shot, the play of light around the forehead, nose, and eyes—and this light display may have been wrought largely in the darkroom. Certainly a photographer can shoot a picture of me which resembles me so little that you won't pick me out. Why deny, then, that when his picture does resemble me, at least some measure of the resemblance is due to how he made the picture?

Then let us not deny it; let us suppose that all characteristics of the photograph, including those which have to do with its status as a representation and a resembler, are there, at least in part—and probably in very large part—because of the efforts of the photographer.

We should, however, note another thing as well. Earlier I said that I do not doubt that when we find parents in their children or subjects in their photographs, we attribute this to something more or other than artifice—call it 'nature.' I also said that I do not know just why we make this attribution. My remarks about parents and children were meant to show that when we do it we do it rather clumsily and out of a kind of prejudice, and that it is unclear what we are saying when we credit nature with my daughter's resemblance to her mother. But we do say it, we do do it. I do it. I admit it. I want to find the implicit content when I say it.

I am looking at a photograph. In it I see my son and his bicycle, among other things. This fact, that I see my son and his Motobecane in there, is due to the fact that *he and the bike were there* when the shot was taken. This is not *a priori.* The fact needn't have been a fact. There are other ways in which a photographic picture which looks much like this one might have been made. And my boy and his bike might have been there, and a photograph have been made which looked so little like this one that you couldn't see the boy and bike in it. So the fact of their being there is not an *a priori* fact, not a necessary fact, and certainly not a fact you could discern with certainty merely by gazing at this photograph. But it is a fact. And the knowledge that it is a fact informs my view of this photograph every instant. It is this quality, this flavor, this phenomenology of viewing photographs which leads people to say that when we look at photographs we look—really look—into the world's past. It may be one of the things that lead Ken Walton to say that we look at the things themselves. It leads us, at least some of us, some times, to prefer to look at a photograph than any other kind of picture.

This may sound like voodoo. (This may *be* voodoo.) But try to keep this epistemology out of it. Maybe I am wrong about the photograph. Maybe it wasn't taken in the summer of 1984. Maybe it's not Amos: it's his twin or a robot or a picture of him. Can I prove that it's him? No. So what? When I look at my daughter, sometimes, it makes all the difference that I know she is my daughter. I know she is my natural daughter, in fact. Can I prove it? Maybe she's the milkman's. Maybe, as she is wont to insist when she is disgusted, she was stolen at birth from a better family and brought to us, and maybe I don't know this. So I look at her as my natural daughter and I am wrong to do so. I can't prove that she is my daughter. So what?

One has faith in photographs, so to speak. It can be misplaced. When photographs are introduced in court, competent attorneys insist on documentation of the provenance of the pictures. They know that a photograph itself, alone, doesn't prove anything. And sometimes, in court and elsewhere, a man might have to try to prove, as they say, beyond a reasonable doubt, that a girl is his daughter. The fact that the man and the girl look alike and have been together virtually all her life—those things themselves, alone, don't prove fatherhood.

Fatherhood is not carried out in court, however, nor are photographs characteristically appreciated there. To see this photograph, of my son and his wheels, as if it were merely contingently, incidentally, insignificantly connected to the fact that once he and it were there, on Dorchester Avenue, is a possible achievement, I suppose. It is, however, an arch aestheticization, a diminution, I think.

Another kind of diminution is achieved by those who view this as the only relevant fact, as if it were trivial that the film was Kodak's MP 5247, ASA 200, that the *f* stop was 8 and the shutter speed 1/250 of a second, and the rest of those things. Drop those things out and *you* are practicing voodoo. If those things weren't as they were, you wouldn't see him in the photograph as you do.

What follows from this? Nothing, I think, in this sense: nothing follows about the character of photography or its aesthetics. There is nothing in this to suggest that photographs are devoid of art; but there is nothing to suggest that their capacity to support nostalgia and their use as a tool against skepticism are illegitimate. The relation of photographs to the world is in some respects more natural than the comparable relation of other pictures. I have said what I can about those respects, and I conclude this section by observing that nothing whatever is implied about whether photographs are art, or have style or can be expressive, or are in those respects different from other pictures.

The alleged special relation of photographs to the world is, allegedly, related to the alleged mechanical or automatic character of photography. What about this machinery? The machine in question, I suppose, is the camera, although the not infrequent reference to things like "optical and chemical" properties suggests that darkroom apparatus involved in developing and printing is to be included. There are two, separate points, and I will take them quickly in turn. The first concerns the fact that there is a machine in the works, the second has to do with the fact that this machine is somehow automatic.

The first point, despite the extent to which it dominates much thinking about photography, has remarkably little substance. It often seems to amount to an obsession with the fact of the camera, with the fact that it is a *machine*. This fact cannot by itself be especially pertinent, because machines are parts of a number of arts. When my son is cleaning and repairing his French horn the parts of this incredible apparatus cover the dining room floor. He plays the horn well, and he has a commendable knowledge of how the thing works. I would guess that his knowledge is comparable in scope to a photographer's knowledge of how his machine works. The difference, some would say, is that the camera is an *automatic* kind of machine and the horn is not that kind of machine. What does that mean? That cameras work all by themselves? They can be made to work by themselves, after a fashion; but if you outfitted the horn with an altered mouthpiece and set it out in a blizzard then it would work by itself. Responding to praise of his performance at the organ, Bach is reported to have said this:

> There is nothing remarkable about it. All one has to do is hit the right notes at the right time, and the instrument plays itself.

A charming remark, but not meant to be taken seriously; and the idea of setting up the French horn in a blizzard is just foolish. Still, I don't see exactly how it is more foolish than the idea that the camera is automatic—when this automatism is cited as an inherently unartistic or uncreative core in photography. With a camera, I suppose one might say, all one has to do is set the aperture and shutter mechanisms, point the thing the right way, hit the shutter button at the right time, and the instrument will play itself, just like Bach's organ.

The significant difference has to do with the results: the camera delivers a picture (at least sometimes), and it might do this, as it were, almost "by chance." Neither a pipe organ nor a French horn is likely to deliver a tune by chance. Let us try to get a grip on this idea that a camera is an automatic picture-making machine. Then we can try to understand why this fact about the camera seems to some to diminish the artistic capacities of photography, and finally I can say why this fact does not do this but does render photographs a special kind of picture.

It is undeniable that photography is automatically in possession of a capacity for a kind of gross, generic representation. By that I mean that with a camera virtually anyone can make easily detected likenesses of things and people. Not many of us can do this without a camera, especially when the task is to make a likeness of a person. In this respect one might say that photographs are infinitely "easier" to make than are other kinds of pictures. But it is only in this respect, and negative consequences for the artistic potential of photographs would follow, if at all, only if they were easier in all other respects. Some people write as if they were.

One way to make a picture which looks like a tall man is to turn your camera on a tall man (and pay some attention to what else shows up in your picture). One way to make a picture which looks like a tall, sad man is to turn your camera on a tall man looking sad. Some writers write as if they thought that were the only way to get sadness into a photograph, indeed as if the only way any of the oft-cited, little-understood values of plastic art—the expression of feeling and emotion, the celebration of life or God or whatever—as if the only way any of that could get into a photograph is by way of the photographer's finding those expressions, celebrations, etc. in the world and turning his camera on them. That idea is so misguided and so wrong that the only interest it yields is wonder at how it can arise. I personally believe it arises either from (1) an abysmal ignorance of the most elementary facts concerning how photographs are made, or (2) a steady diet of examples in each of which something like a family-album snapshot is compared with something like a Velazquez or a Rembrandt. Or it arises from the ignorance plus the stacked examples, perhaps because the ignorance leads one to choose just such pairs of examples.

A photograph might be profoundly sad and yet show a happy-looking person, or the other way round. A photograph might be "about" the isolation of a person from others, the insignificance of people, the triumph of the will, the eternal newness of America, the impossibility of the marriage contract. Of course it might, it could be about any of those things. And the photographer's problem in making such a photograph would be exactly the same as any picture-maker's, except, of course, that he has to address the problem in terms of the resources of photography, which are not the same as those of oil painting, but they do not make his task easier, nor do they make it impossible.

The picture we seem to be stuck with is this. Suppose *M* [a maker] makes something, *X*. Suppose *L* [a looker] looks at *X*. The question is, how does the relation of *M* to *X* compare with the relation of *L* to *X*? There seem to be two extreme cases, one in which the relations have to be the same, and one in which they cannot be the same. We are tempted to believe that photography is an instance of the first case, and painting an example of the second. In the second case *M* must have had a pre-conception of *X* in order to make *X*, and therefore his relation to it is different from that of *L*, who has no conception of *X* until he sees it. (This pre-conception is what, in the *Critique of Judgement,* Kant calls a *Zweck.*) That is to say, for instance, that the painter has to know what he's going to do before he does it. This contrasts with the first case, where photography is supposed to belong, in which *M* needs no prior conceptualizing but makes do with a camera, something to point it at, and some light to reflect off whatever he's pointing at. He need have no efficacious conception, and so his photograph can be his occasion for the conception just as it is *L*'s. (This is why it seems unremarkable when a photographer *discovers* what is in his own picture.)

This way of thinking of things leaves very little room for artistry on the part of the photographer. There certainly are photographs like this, ones about which, had you noticed where the camera was aimed, you would have as good an idea as the photographer how the picture would look. But if the photographer is able, and especially if he is very good, you won't know how his picture will look, not even if you look through the viewfinder. Or, to put it better, the things you do know are precisely not the things that will matter most.

The things you do know about what the photograph is likely to look like are, on the whole, exactly those things that will appear because of photography's automatic capacity for what I am calling gross depiction—the achievement of easily recognized likenesses. My idea is that this achievement dislocates the value of representation, especially relative to its value in other kinds of pictures. It is an old idea that photography freed painting from the burden of representing. I think this old idea is backwards. It is photography which is freed of this burden, just because it is no *burden* in photography. Contrary to Susan Sontag, for instance, I think that one's informed attention when looking at photographs tends to go elsewhere than to what is (grossly) depicted. . . .

Neither the intimate relation of photographs to reality (such as that relation may be), nor the mechanical character of the camera is a bar to art in photography. It follows that there is no need for those who find photography artistic to deny either of these things. And it would be a mistake to do so. In the fist place, as difficult as it is to describe the intimate relation, and as annoying as it is to be forced to say what's different in photography's automatism that would distinguish it from any other art's machinery, these are special, unique features of photography. In the second place, these features endow photographs with specials interest which may or may not have to do with *Art.* . . .

Take my photograph of my son. . . . [T]his picture is no work of art, or at least it is not one of consequence. It is, however, of considerable value to me; and I dearly hope that someday it will touch him as what it is, or was meant to be, my attempt to make sense for him and me of the day of a city boy and his bike in the summer—an attempt to create his day.

Only a photograph could do this for us, because, unlike a painting, it signals that he was there and I was there and we were together making this photograph. Photographs can do such things for us. They can also be art. Perhaps in some cases their artistry incorporates this value of intimacy in the past preserved, this sense of the object and the photographer united in this picture. I think this of some things by Atget and some by Walker Evans. In those pictures I sense the choice of the photographer, the selection of something with which to unite. But this is all very flighty (as my friendly critic Joel Snyder would say, I have left the ground). Let me conclude, therefore, by concluding that there is nothing whatever in the nature of photography which disqualifies it as art, and by speculating that there are things in its nature which make it—some of the time—one of the kinds of art it can be.

Allegory of the Cave

Plato

And now, I said, let me show in a figure how far our nature is enlightened or unenlightened:—Behold! human beings living in an underground den, which has a mouth open towards the light and reaching all along the den; here they have been from their childhood, and have their legs and necks chained so that they cannot move, and can only see before them, being prevented by the chains from turning round their heads. Above and behind them a fire is blazing at a distance, and between the fire and the prisoners there is a raised way; and you will see, if you look, a low wall built along the way, like the screen which marionette players have in front of them, over which they show the puppets.

I see.

And do you see, I said, men passing along the wall carrying all sorts of vessels, and statues and figures of animals made of wood and stone and various materials, which appear over the wall? Some of them are talking, others silent.

You have shown me a strange image, and they are strange prisoners.

An excerpt

Like ourselves, I replied; and they see only their own shadows, or the shadows of one another, which the fire throws in the opposite wall of the cave?

True, he said; how could they see anything but the shadows if they were never allowed to move their heads?

And of the objects which are being carried in like manner they would only see the shadows?

Yes, he said.

And if they were able to converse with one another, would they not suppose that they were naming what was actually before them?

Very true.

And suppose further that the prison had an echo which came from the other side, would they not be sure to fancy when one of the passers-by spoke that the voice which they heard came from the passing shadow?

No question, he replied.

To them, I said, the truth would be literally nothing but the shadows of the images.

That is certain.

And now look again, and see what will naturally follow if the prisoners are released and disabused of their error. At first, when any of them is liberated and compelled suddenly to stand up and turn his neck round and walk and look towards the light, he will suffer sharp pains; the glare will distress him, and he will be unable to see the realities of which in his former state he had seen the shadows; and then conceive some one saying to him, that what he saw before was an illusion, but that now, when he is approaching nearer to being and his eye is turned towards more real existence, he has a clearer vision—what will be his reply? And you may further imagine that his instructor is pointing to the objects as they pass and requiring him to name them—will he not be perplexed? Will he not fancy that the shadows which he formerly saw are truer than the objects which are now shown to him?

Far truer.

And if he is compelled to look straight at the light, will he not have a pain in his eyes which will make him turn away to take refuge in the objects of vision which he can see, and which he will conceive to be in reality clearer than the things which are now being shown to him?

True, he said.

And suppose once more, that he is reluctantly dragged up a steep and rugged ascent, and held fast until he is forced into the presence of the sun himself, is he not likely to be pained and irritated? When he approaches the light his eyes will be dazzled, and he will not be able to see anything at all of what are now called realities.

Not all in a moment, he said.

He will require to grow accustomed to the sight of the upper world. And first he will see the shadows best, next the reflections of men and other objects in the water, and then the objects themselves; then he will gaze upon the light of the moon and the stars and the spangled heaven; and he will see the sky and the stars by night better than the sun or the light of the sun by day?

Certainly.

Last of all he will be able to see the sun, and not mere reflections of him in the water, but he will see him in his own proper place, and not in another; and he will contemplate him as he is.

Certainly.

He will then proceed to argue that this is he who gives the season and the years, and is the guardian of all that is in the visible world, and in a certain way the cause of all things which he and his fellows have been accustomed to behold?

Clearly, he said, he would first see the sun and then reason about him.

And when he remembered his old habitation, and the wisdom of the den and his fellow-prisoners, do you not suppose that he would felicitate himself on the change, and pity them?

Certainly, he would.

And if they were in the habit of conferring honours among themselves on those who were quickest to observe the passing shadows and to remark which of them went before, and which followed after, and which were together; and who were therefore best able to draw conclusions as to the future, do you think that he would care for such honours and glories, or envy the possessors of them? Would he not say with Homer,

'Better to be the poor servant of a poor master,' and to endure anything, rather than think as they do and live after their manner?

Yes, he said, I think that he would rather suffer anything than entertain these false notions and live in this miserable manner.

Imagine once more, I said, such a one coming suddenly out of the sun to be replaced in his old situation; would he not be certain to have his eyes full of darkness?

To be sure, he said.

And if there were a contest, and he had to compete in measuring the shadows with the prisoners who had never moved out of the den, while his sight was still weak, and before his eyes had become steady (and the time which would be needed to acquire this new habit of sight might be very considerable), would he not be ridiculous? Men would say of him that up he went and down he came without his eyes; and that it was better not even to think of ascending; and if any one tried to loose another and lead him up to the light, let them only catch the offender, and they would put him to death.

No question, he said.

This entire allegory, I said, you may now append, dear Glaucon, to the previous argument; the prison-house is the world of sight, the light of the fire is the sun, and you will not misapprehend me if you interpret the journey upwards to be the ascent of the soul into the intellectual world according to my poor belief, which, at your desire, I have expressed—whether rightly or wrongly God knows. But, whether true or false, my opinion is that in the world of knowledge the idea of good appears last of all, and is seen only with an effort; and, when seen, is also inferred to be the universal author of all things beautiful and right, parent of light and of the lord of light in this visible world, and the immediate source of reason and truth in the intellectual; and that this is the power upon which he who would act rationally either in public or private life must have his eye fixed. . . .

The Power of Movies

Noël Carroll

. . . Given that the typical movie image is a pictorial representation, what has this to do with accessibility? Well, a picture is a very special sort of symbol. Psychological evidence strongly supports the contention that we learn to recognize what a picture stands for as soon as we have become able to recognize the objects, or kinds of objects, that serve as the models for that picture. Picture recognition is not a skill acquired over and above object recognition. Whatever features or cues we come to employ in object recognition, we also mobilize to recognize what pictures depict. A child raised without pictorial representations will, after being shown a couple of pictures, be able to identify the referent of any picture of an object with which he or she is familiar. The rapid development of this picture-recognition capacity contrasts strongly with the acquisition of a symbol system such as language. Upon mastering a couple of words, the child is nowhere near mastering the entire language. Similarly, when an adult is exposed to one or two representational *pictures* in an alien pictorial idiom, say a Westerner confronting a Japanese image in the floating-point-of-view style, he will be able to identify the referent of any picture in that format after studying one or two representations of that sort for a few moments. But no Westerner, upon learning one or two linguistic symbols of the Japanese language, could go on to identify the reference of all, or even merely a few more, Japanese words. Moreover, historically the Japanese were eminently able to catch on to and replicate the Western system of perspectival picturing by examining a selection of book illustrations; but they could never have acquired any European language by learning the meanings of just a few words or phrases. . . .

We have explained why movies are more accessible than genres like novels. But what features of movies account for their presumably superior accessibility and intensity in comparison with media and genres like drama, ballet, and opera, in which recognition of what the representations refer to is, like movies, typically not mediated by learned processes of decoding, reading, or inference? What standard features of movies differentiate them from the standard features of the presentation of plays, for example, in a way that make typical movies more accessible than typical theatrical performances? . . .

Of course, movies and standard theatrical productions share many of the same devices for directing the audience's attention. Both in the medium-long shot and on the proscenium stage, the audience's attention can be guided by: the central positioning of an important character; movement in stasis; stasis in movement; characters' eye-

---

An excerpt

lines; light colors on dark fields; dark colors on light fields; sound, notably dialogue; spotlighting and variable illumination of the array; placement of important objects or characters along arresting diagonals; economy of set details; makeup and costume; commentary; gestures; and so on. But movies appear to have further devices and perhaps more effective devices for directing attention than does theater as it is presently practiced. The variability of focus in film, for example, is a more reliable means of making sure that the audience is looking where the spectator "ought" to be looking than is theatrical lighting. Even more important is the use in movies of variable framing. Through cutting and camera movement, the filmmaker can rest assured that the spectator is perceiving exactly what she should be perceiving at the precise moment she should be perceiving it. When the camera comes in for a close-up, for example, there is no possibility that the spectator can be distracted by some detail stage-left. Everything extraneous to the story at that point is deleted. Nor does the spectator have to find the significant detail; it is delivered to her. The viewer also gets as close or as far-off a view of the significant objects of the story—be they heroines, butcher knives, mobs, fortresses, or planets—as is useful for her to have a concrete sense of what is going on. Whereas in a theater the eye constantly tracks the action—often at a felt distance, often amidst a vaulting space—in movies much of that work is done by shifting camera positions, which at the same time also assures that the average viewer has not gotten lost in the space but is looking precisely at that which she is supposed to see. Movies are therefore easier to follow than typical stage productions, because the shifting camera positions make it practically impossible for the movie viewer *not* to be attending where she is meant to attend.

Variable framing in film is achieved by moving the camera closer or farther away from the objects being filmed. Cutting and camera movement are the two major processes for shifting framing: in the former, the actual process of the camera's change of position is not included in the shot; we jump from medium-range views, to close views, to far-off views with the traversal of the space between excised; in camera movement, as the name suggests, the passage of the camera from a long view to a close view is recording within the shot. Reframing can also be achieved optically through devices such as zooming-in and changing lenses. These mechanical means for changing the framing of an on-screen object or event give rise to three formal devices for directing the movie audience's attention: indexing, bracketing, and scaling. Indexing occurs when a camera is moved toward an object. The motion toward the object functions ostensively, like the gesture of pointing. It indicates that the viewer ought to be looking in the direction the camera is moving, if the camera's movement is being recorded, or in the direction toward which the camera is aimed or pointing, if we have been presented with the shot via a cut.

When a camera is moved towards an array, it screens out everything beyond the frame. To move a camera toward an object either by cutting or camera movement generally has the force of indicating that what is important at this moment is what is on screen, what is in the perimeter of the frame. That which is not inside the frame has been *bracketed,* excluded. It should not, and in fact it literally cannot, at the moment it is bracketed, be attended to. At the same time, bracketing has an inclusionary dimension, indicating that what is inside the frame or bracket is important. A standard camera position will mobilize both the exclusionary and inclusionary dimensions of the bracket to control attention, though the relative degree may vary as to whether a given bracketing is more important for what it excludes, rather than what it includes, and vice-versa.

There is also a standard deviation from this use of bracketing. Often the important element of a scene is placed outside the frame so that it is not visible onscreen, e.g., the child-killer in the early part of Fritz Lang's *M.* Such scenes derive a great deal of their expressive power just because they subvert the standard function of bracketing.

As the camera is moved forward, it not only indexes and places brackets around the objects in front of it; it also changes their scale. Whether by cutting or camera movement, as the camera nears the gun on the table, the gun simultaneously appears larger and occupies more screen space. When the camera is pulled away from the table, the gun occupies less screen space. This capacity to change the scale of objects through camera positioning—a process called "scaling"—can be exploited for expressive or magical effects. Scaling is also a lever for directing attention. Enlarging the screen size of an object generally has the force of stating that this object, or gestalt of objects, is the important item to attend to at this moment in the movie.

Scaling, bracketing, and indexing are three different ways of directing the movie spectator's attention through camera positioning. In general, a standard camera positioning, whether executed by cutting or camera movement, will employ all three of these means. . . .

So far, our speculations about the sources of the power of movies have been restricted to what would have classically been considered the medium's "cinematic features": pictorial representation and variable framing. This, of course, does not reflect a belief that these elements are uniquely cinematic, but only that they are features that help account for movies' power, the capacity to engender what appears to be an unprecedentedly widespread and intense level of engagement. There is another core defining features of what we are calling movies that needs to be treated: this is that they are fictional narratives. The question naturally arises to what degree this fact about movies can help explain their power.

The fact that movies tend to be narrative, concerned primarily with depictions of human actions, immediately suggests one of the reasons they are accessible. For narrative is, in all probability, our most pervasive and familiar means of explaining human action. . . .

A story film will portray a sequence of scenes or events, some appearing earlier, some later. A practical problem that confronts the filmmaker is the way in which these scenes are to be connected, i.e., what sort of relation the earlier scenes should bear to the later ones. [V.I.] Pudovkin recommends—as a primary, though not exclusive, solution—that earlier scenes be related to later scenes as questions are to answers. If a giant shark appears offshore, unbeknownst to the local authorities, and begins to ravage lonely swimmers, this scene or series of scenes (or this event or series of events) raises the question of whether the shark will ever be detected. This question is likely to be answered in some later scene when someone figures out why all those swimmers are missing. At that point, when it is learnt that the shark is very, very powerful and nasty to boot, the question arises about whether it can be destroyed or driven away. The ensuing events in the film serve to answer that question. Or, if some atomic bombs are sky-jacked in the opening scenes, this generates questions about who stole them and for what purposes. Once the generally nefarious purposes of the hijacking are established, the question arises concerning whether these treacherous intents can be thwarted. Or, for a slightly more complicated scenario, shortly after a jumbo jet takes off, we learn that the entire crew has just died from food poisoning while also learning that the couple in first class is estranged. These scenes raise the questions of whether the plane will crash and whether the couple in first class will be reconciled by their common ordeal. Maybe we also ask whether the alcoholic priest in coach will find God again. It is the function of the later scenes in the film to answer these questions. . . .

Thus, to narrate by generating questions internal to the film that subsequent scenes answer is a distinctive form of narration. Admittedly, this is not a form unique to films or movies, for it is also exploited in mystery novels, adventure stories, Harlequin romances, Marvel comics, and so on. Nevertheless, it is the most characteristic narrative approach in movies.

How can this be proven? The best suggestion one can make here is to embrace the question/answer model of movie narration—what I call the *erotetic* model of narrative—and then turn on your TV, watch old movies and new ones, TV adventure series and romances, domestic films and foreign popular films. Ask yourself why the later scenes in the films make sense in the context of the earlier scenes. My prediction is that you will be surprised by the extent to which later scenes are answering questions raised earlier, or are at least providing information that will contribute to such answers. In adopting the hypothesis that the narrative structure of a randomly selected movie is fundamentally a system of internally generated questions that the movie goes on to answer, you will find that you have hold of a relationship that enables you to explain what makes certain scenes especially key: they either raise questions or answer them, or perform related functions including sustaining questions already raised, or incompletely answering a previous question, or answering one question but then introducing a new one. . . .

A successful erotetic narrative tells you, literally, everything you want to know about the action being depicted, i.e., it answers every question, or virtually every question, that it has chosen to pose saliently. (I say "virtually" in order to accommodate endings such as that in the original *Invasion of the Body Snatchers,* where the audience is left with one last pregnant question.) But even countenancing these cases, an erotetic movie narrative has an extraordinary degree of neatness and intellectually appealing compactness. It answers all the questions that it assertively presents to the audience, and the largest portion of its actions is organized by a small number of macro-questions, with little remainder. The flow of action approaches an ideal of uncluttered clarity. This clarity contrasts vividly with the quality of the fragments of actions and events we typically observe in everyday life. Unlike those in real life, the actions observed in movies have a level of intelligibility, due to the role they play in the erotetic narrative's system of questions and answers. Because of the question/answer structure, the audience is left with the impression that it has learned everything important to know concerning the action depicted. How is this achieved? By assertively introducing a selected set of pressing questions and then answering them—by controlling expectation by the manner in which questions are posed. This imbues the film with an aura of clarity while also affording an intense satisfaction concerning our cognitive expectations and our propensity for intelligibility. . . .

We began by addressing the issue of the power of movies, which was understood as a question concerning the ways in which movies have engaged the widespread, intense response of untutored audiences throughout the century. We have dealt with the issue of the widespread response to movies by pointing to those features of movies that make them particularly accessible. We have also dealt with our intense engagement with movies in terms of the impression of coherence they impart, i.e., their easily grasped, indeed, their almost unavoidable, clarity. The accessibility of movies is at least attributable to their use of pictorial representation, variable framing, and narrative, the latter being the most pervasive form of explaining human actions. Their clarity is at least a function of variable framing in coordination with the erotetic narrative, especially where erotetic narration and variable framing are coordinated by the principle that the first item or gestalt of items the audience apprehends be that which, out of alternative framings, is most important to the narration. In short, this thesis holds that the power of movies—their capacity to evoke unrivaled widespread and intense response—is, first and foremost, at least a result of their deployment of pictorial representation, variable framing, and the erotetic narrative. . . .

The Expression and Arousal of Emotion in Music

Jenefer Robinson

. . . According to some theories of musical expression, the grounds on which we attribute expressive qualities to music have nothing to do with the arousal of emotion in the audience. According to Peter Kivy's account in *The Corded Shell,* a musical element such as a melody, a rhythm, or a chord expresses a feeling not because it arouses that feeling in anyone but for two quite different reasons. (1) It has the same "contour" as expressive human behavior of some kind and thus is "heard as expressive of something or other because heard as appropriate to the expression of something or other"

An excerpt

(for example, the "weeping" figure of grief in Arianna's lament from Monteverdi's *Arianna*) or it contributes in a particular context to the forming of such an expressive contour (as the diminished triad in a suitable context can contribute to a *restless* quality in the music, although all by itself it does not express anything). (2) The musical element is expressive by virtue of some custom or convention, which originated in connection with some expressive contour. The minor triad, for example, is "sad" by convention, although it may have started life as part of some expressive contour.

There are many examples of musical expression for which Kivy's argument is convincing. Thus it does seem to be true that Arianna's lament mirrors the passionate speaking voice expressing grief, that Schubert's "Gretchen am Spinnrad" mirrors Gretchen's monotonous, leaden gestures at the spinning wheel and her correspondingly dejected, leaden heart, and that the "Pleni sunt coeli" from Bach's B Minor Mass maps "bodily motion and gesture . . . of tremendous expansiveness, vigor, violent motion," thus mirroring the exuberance of " 'leaping' joy." At the same time as Renée Cox, among others, has pointed out, virtually all the musical examples in Kivy's book are examples of music with a text, and it is relatively uncontroversial that a text can specify a particular feeling or object which is characterized by the music. Moreover, when we look closely at Kivy's examples of particular emotions said to be expressed by music we find mainly varieties of joy, sorrow, and restlessness. The vast majority of musical examples in *The Corded Shell* can be characterized as expressions of either positive or negative emotion (joy or sorrow) of various sorts. Thus although what Kivy says seems to be true as far as it goes, it does not go very far, and leaves a great deal of expressiveness in music unexplained.

Kivy holds that music can express particular emotional states such as sorrow and joy, restlessness and serenity. Susanne Langer, while agreeing that emotional qualities are to be found in the *music,* rather than in the *listener,* follows Hanslick in arguing that since only the dynamic qualities of anything (including emotional states) can be expressed by music, no particular emotions can be expressed by music, but only the felt quality of our emotional life and its dynamic development:

> [There] are certain aspects of the so-called "inner life"—physical or mental—which have formal properties similar to those of music—patterns of motion and rest, of tension and release, of agreement and disagreement, preparation, fulfillment, excitation, sudden change, etc.
>
> [Music] reveals the rationale of feelings, the rhythm and pattern of their rise and decline and intertwining, to our minds. . . .

In contrast to Kivy's view that the words of a text supply the "fine shadings" to otherwise only grossly expressive musical meanings, Langer holds that musical meanings are inherently rich and significant yet cannot be linked to any particular words. Langer's theory emphasizes the development of structures of feeling throughout a lengthy piece of music, which Kivy ignores, but she in turn ignores the expression of particular emotional qualities which Kivy emphasizes. Both theorists have insightful things to say about musical expression but neither tells the whole story.

A very different view of musical expression has recently been presented by Kendall Walton in a paper called "What Is Abstract About the Art of Music?" Walton proposes that one important way in which music is expressive is by virtue of the fact that in listening to music we imagine ourselves introspecting, being aware of, our own feelings. As he puts it, we imagine "of our actual introspective awareness of auditory sensations" that "it is an experience of being aware of our states of mind." Thus the expressiveness of music has to do with its power to *evoke* certain imaginative emotional experiences. Moreover, Walton says that if this is right, then:

> music probably can be said to "portray particulars" in the sense that figurative paintings do, rather than simply properties or concepts. Presumably the listener imagines experiencing and identifying *particular* stabs of pain, *particular* feelings of ecstasy, *particular* sensations of well-being, etc., as in viewing a painting one imagines seeing particular things.

However, whereas one perceives the psychological states of other people, as in figurative paintings, one "introspects one's *own* psychological states."

There are at least two problems I see with Walton's account. (1) First, suppose someone denies that this is what she does when listening to expressive music; we should be able to *explain* to her why this is what she should be doing. What reason is there why we should imagine our awareness of auditory sensations—experienced sequences of musical tones—to be an experience of our feelings and other inner states? True, there are similarities between the two: the experience of auditory sensations is an introspectible state, and so is awareness of our feelings. True, part of what we are aware of in these auditory sensations is, as Langer points out, their ebb and flow, and our feelings too have ebb and flow. But beyond these points of resemblance there seems to be little explanation *why* we should be inclined to imagine our awareness of musical sounds to be an awareness of our feelings. Imagination requires some guidance if it is not to be merely free association: I can imagine the tree at the end of the garden to be a witch because it has a witch-like appearance, but it is unclear what it would mean for me to imagine the snowdrop at my feet to be a witch if there is nothing about the snowdrop to set off my imagination. Similarly, in order for me to imagine my awareness of musical sounds to be awareness of my feelings, something in the musical sounds must guide my imagination. However, if the only points of resemblance between feelings and sounds is introspectibility and ebb and flow, then I would suggest that this is insufficient to ground an imaginative identification between the two. There are, moreover, striking *differences* between the two which would seem to preclude any such imaginative identification. In particular, whereas our feelings clearly rise up inside us (as we say), musical sounds as clearly rise up at a distance from us: even when listening to music over good earphones—when the music is experienced with peculiar immediacy—we still experience the auditory sensations as coming from an external source, such as trombones and the like. That is why although we can perhaps imagine these sounds as feelings welling up inside the *composer,* or perhaps in some *character* described by the music, it is not obvious to me that we can imagine them as feelings welling up inside ourselves.

(2) There is a second problem related to this one. I am willing to grant that there are indeed movements in music which it is appropriate to call "stabbing" or "surging."

According to Walton, however, the music induces me to imagine myself feeling a particular ecstatic surge or stab of pain. He says that the music *portrays* these particulars (it picks them out or refers to them). A number of questions need to be distinguished here. (1) Can the stab be identified as a stab of feeling rather than the stab of a dagger or some other kind of stab? (2) If the stab is a stab of feeling, can it be identified as a stab of pain rather than some other feeling such as excitement or jealousy? (3) If the stab is indeed a stab of pain, can it be identified as a stab of pain which I imagine myself experiencing rather than a stab of pain attributed to someone else such as Othello or the composer? If the music *portrays* my imagined stab of pain, as Walton suggests, then the music must be able to distinguish my imagined stab of pain from all these other possible alternatives. Can music do this? Can music portray this particular stab of pain and no other? . . .

Although Walton's theory does not identify musical expression with the straightforward arousal of feelings, he does try to explain expression in terms of the arousal of *imaginary* feelings. I am not actually feeling a stab of pain as I listen to the stabbing music; I am *imagining* experiencing a stab of pain, so it would seem that the pain is an imaginary feeling. In his paper "Music and Negative Emotions," Jerrold Levinson makes a similar point. Levinson's paper deals with the problem of why people enjoy music when it evokes negative emotions such as sadness in them. While the paper does not develop a theory of musical expression, it does make certain assumptions about what often happens when people listen to music which we would characterize as sad. In particular, he assumes that it is a normal response for people to have a sadness-reaction to music.

When a person has a "deep emotional response" to music, this is "generally in virtue of the *recognition* of emotions expressed in music," but recognition then leads to a kind of empathic identification: we "end up feeling as, in imagination, the music does." Such empathic emotional responses to music consist in "something very like experience of the emotion expressed in the music" but not *exactly* like it. In both cases the physiological and affective components of emotion are present and in both cases there is cognitive content, but the "empathic" response lacks *determinate* cognitive content:

> When one hears sad music, begins to feel sad, and imagines that one is actually sad, one must, according to the logic of the concept, be imagining that there is an object for one's sadness and that one maintains certain evaluative beliefs (or attitudes) regarding it. The point, though, is that this latter imagining generally remains indeterminate.

I feel sad but my sadness has no determinate object; it is directed only to "some featureless object posited vaguely by my imagination." Levinson illustrates his view with various kinds of negative emotion: "intense grief, unrequited passion, sobbing melancholy, tragic resolve, and angry despair." Suppose, for example, that the music evokes in me an empathic response of unrequited passion. On Levinson's view, this means that I recognize unrequited passion in the music, I imagine that I am experiencing unrequited passion, and I actually experience the physiological and affective components of unrequited passion. My imagined unrequited passion has a cognitive content which is "etiolated by comparison to that of real-life emotion"; however, I am not really suffering the pangs of unrequited passion, and in particular there is no special person for whom I am languishing.

I am sympathetic to some of Levinson's assumptions: I think he is right to stress that the detection of emotional qualities in music has something to do with the arousal of emotion by music, and I think he is right also to stress the role of the imagination in the appreciation of emotional qualities in music. However, the theory as it stands will not do. First of all, it is far from clear that every emotional state has identifiable physiological and affective components. For example, real-life unrequited passion might on different occasions be accompanied by a great variety of inner feelings (love, grief, longing, jealousy, wretchedness, despair, self-contempt, etc., etc.). For another thing, the particular feelings I experience on a given occasion of unrequited passion may be just the same as I have felt on occasions of angry despair or intense grief. The truth of the matter is that there may be very little difference between the affective and physiological components of very different emotions: I may feel the same mixture of grief and rage when I am jealous or when I am grieving (without jealousy); I may have very similar feelings whether angrily despairing, tragically resolving, or suffering from the pangs of unrequited passion. The difference between these emotions lies not so much in their affective and physiological components as in their cognitive content. The chief difference between unrequited passion, tragic resolve, and angry despair is how I view or conceive of the situation.

But now we come to a second set of difficulties. Levinson argues that I can recognize unrequited passion (say) in the "emotion-laden gestures embodied in musical movement" and by virtue of this recognition respond emphatically with feelings of unrequited passion of my own, since I identify with the music or perhaps "with the person whom we imagine owns the emotions or emotional gestures we hear in the music." However, he fails to tell us how we detect or empathically feel the unrequited passion in the music. Although we all have some idea of what *sad* music is like, I suggest that it is much less clear what a piece of music is like in which we can recognize, and hence empathize with, unrequited passion (always assuming, of course, that there is no accompanying verbal text to help us out). If I am right and there are no distinctive affective or physiological components of unrequited passion, then the obvious way to clarify the nature of music in which we can detect unrequited passion would be to specify its cognitive content. Now, Levinson claims that the cognitive content of an emotional response to music is normally "etiolated." This could mean simply that my imagined feelings of unrequited passion are not directed to any particular individual. While it is a little odd to say that one can feel unrequited passion for someone I know not whom, we can perhaps make sense of this suggestion since on Levinson's view the unrequited passion I feel empathically belongs to the music itself or to someone whom we imagine feels unrequited passion, so that we merely empathize with this imagined person's unrequited passion.

Even if we grant, however, that there need be no specific object for the unrequited passion I detect in the music and empathize with, it would seem that there must be some identifiable cognitive content, however etiolated, which is detectable in the music in order to justify the attribution of this particular emotion. I would suggest that if my response is to count as a response of unrequited passion rather than some other emotion, then I must imagine that there is someone whom I care about deeply, that this person does not care deeply about me, and that I care deeply that this person does not care deeply about me (or something of this sort). It is a serious problem for Levinson's account that he does not tell us how such conceptions can be embodied in music and hence how we can either recognize or empathize with the corresponding emotion. We find the same problem with tragic resolve and angry despair; we cannot clearly distinguish these emotional responses by their affective and physiological components alone, but only by their cognitive content. However, Levinson gives us no clue as to how their cognitive content can be recognized in or induced by music. . . .

Recently Levinson's view has been criticized by Peter Kivy on the grounds that the expression of emotion in music is entirely independent of the arousal of that emotion. Kivy argues that to have one's emotions aroused by a piece of music—in particular, to be moved by a piece of music—is quite distinct from perceiving a particular emotional quality in that piece. Music that is sad or expresses sadness is music with a sad expressive contour or music that is sad by convention, not music that arouses or evokes sadness. Levinson argues that a "deep emotional response" to sad music consists in the arousal of a kind of imaginative but cognitively truncated sadness. Kivy rightly attacks this claim, arguing on the one hand that sad music may or may not make me feel anything, depending on how great the music is (the "yards and yards of mournful music" written by Telemann may fail to make me feel anything much at all), and on the other hand that there are important emotions aroused by music which are full-blown, ordinary, real-life emotions, not "truncated" or "imaginary" in any sense. He illustrates his point by reference to a performance of Josquin's "Ave verum virginitas" which, he says *moves* him deeply.

When listening to the "Ave verum virginitas" I may simply be moved by "the sheer beauty of the sound as it unfolds in its ebb and flow." If my sophistication increases, however, I may also be moved by "the incomparable beauty and craftsmanship of Josquin's counterpoint" and by the fact that despite its seeming effortlessness, the music is written in a particularly difficult canonic form, "a canon at the fifth, with the voices only one beat apart." This, then, is the cognitive component of the emotion aroused by the music, my being moved by the music. It is not a truncated emotion in any way. It is a genuine emotional experience, arising out of my perception of the music and its qualities. Furthermore, this emotion might be directed at emotional, expressive qualities in the music, such as sadness, but it does not follow that the emotion *aroused by* the music is the emotion *detected in* the music. Part of what I may be moved by in a piece of music may be its sadness, but I can be moved by joyful, by energetic, and by serene music just as well, as well as by music which does not have any marked emotional character. The expressive qualities, if any, which I detect in the music are entirely independent of the emotions I feel as I listen to the music.

Now, Kivy is certainly right to claim that when I am moved by a piece of music, my emotion may be independent of the emotional qualities, if any, that the music happens to have. When I appreciate a piece of music I may indeed be moved in the way Kivy describes. On the other hand, Kivy has not succeeded in showing that the expression of emotion by a piece of music is always and entirely unconnected to the arousal of emotion. Kivy makes this claim based on an analysis of just one emotion, "being moved," and it may well be true that we can be equally moved by music with different emotional qualities, as well as by music which has no marked emotional qualities. However, I believe that music arouses other feelings as well and that some of these may indeed be connected to the expressive qualities that music has. Furthermore, I think Kivy is wrong to insist that *all* the feelings aroused by music have to have a complex cognitive component as in his example from Josquin. It may be true that being moved by music involves complex evaluative judgments, but being moved is not the only emotional or feeling response which music can arouse.

Let me summarize the results of my discussion so far. Walton argues that expressive music evokes the imaginative experience of the emotion expressed: more precisely, music expressive of sadness, say, induces the listener to imagine herself experiencing sad feelings. Levinson similarly claims that sad music has the power to evoke a kind of truncated sadness-response: the listener feels certain symptoms of sadness, has an "indeterminate" idea that there is something or other to be sad about and imagines that she in fact feels sad. Both writers find a connection between the presence of an emotional quality in music and the arousal of that emotion in the listener's imagination. I have urged, however, that neither Walton nor Levinson has shown *how* complex feelings such as unrequited passion, stabs of pain, or even sadness can be aroused by music whether in fact or in imagination. Furthermore, Kivy is clearly right to hold that to have a deep emotional response to music is not necessarily to mirror the feelings that the music expresses.

At the same time, however, I believe that Walton and Levinson are right to stress the connection between the expression and the arousal of emotion in music, and that Kivy is quite wrong to think that his analysis of the one emotion "being moved" demonstrates that no such connection exists. In what remains of this paper I will try to sketch a more adequate account of what this connection really is.

None of the writers I have discussed in this essay has focused on the way in which music can *directly* affect our feelings. For both Walton and Levinson the arousal of feeling is imaginative and it relies on a good deal of cognitive activity on the part of the listener. For Kivy the emotion of being moved is a real emotion, not an imagined one, but it too relies on cognitive activity, such as recognizing the clever part-writing, etc. However, some music has the power to affect our feelings without much, if any cognitive mediation. In particular, music can induce physiological changes and a certain quality of inner feeling (what Levinson calls respectively the "phenomenological" and "sensational" aspects of the "affective" component in emotion). Music can make me feel tense or relaxed; it can disturb, unsettle, and startle me; it can calm me down or excite me; it can get me tapping my foot, singing along, or dancing; it can maybe lift my spirits and mellow me out.

Emotions vary in degree—and perhaps in kind—of cognitive content. At one end of the scale there is the startle response, which is an innate response, found in human neonates as well as throughout the phylogenetic scale. At the other end of the scale there is unrequited passion which, by contrast, is found only in humans with their highly developed cultural norms. What I want to suggest is that in addition to the sophisticated emotions of appreciation, which Kivy identifies as "being moved" by certain perceived aspects of the music, there are more primitive emotions aroused by music, perhaps requiring less developed cognitive mediation. There are, after all, moments in music which make us jump or startle us. Similarly, the perception of certain rhythms may be enough—without any further cognitive mediation—to evoke tension or relaxation, excitement or calm. If the melodic and harmonic elements in a piece of music affect our emotions, this would seem to require familiarity with the stylistic norms of the piece, but no further cognitions need be required in order for us to feel soothed, unsettled, surprised, or excited by developments in the music. Certainly we need not notice that we are listening to a canon at the fifth in order for that canon to soothe us.

We have seen that to feel unrequited passion necessarily involves a certain fairly complicated conception of one's situation. By contrast, to feel disturbed or calm does not require having a conception of one's situation in this way. Music can make me feel disturbed or calm just by perceiving it (listening to it). The feeling is a result of a perception and to this extent it has "cognitive content," but it is not the full-blown cognitive content required for tragic resolve, angry despair or unrequited passion. The sense of relaxation we feel at the end of "Tristan und Isolde," for example, is the result of the long-awaited resolution, after over four hours of constant modulation without resolution. The feeling is the result of a perception, but we may not even be aware why we feel as we do: the effect of the constantly shifting harmonic pattern affects us "directly" without conscious cognitive mediation (except, of course, what is required by our understanding of Wagner's style). There is some psychological evidence (from Berlyne and others) that people seek high levels of arousal in order to have them drop afterwards: "excitement and complex, conflicting information are sought because of the 'arousal jag.' " The effect of the final Tristan chord may be partly accounted for in these terms.

Now, the feelings evoked "directly" by music explain some of the cases of musical expressiveness that the contour theory finds hard to deal with. Music that disturbs and unsettles us is disturbing, unsettling music. Modulations that surprise us are surprising. Melodies that soothe us are soothing. Furthermore, unexpected harmonic shifts excite us and are exciting; protracted stay in a harmonic area distant from the home key makes us uneasy and produces uneasy music; the return to the home key after a protracted stay in a distant harmonic area relaxes the tension in us and produces relaxing music. And so on. In short, as against Kivy's position, it seems to me that the expression of a feeling by music can sometimes be explained straightforwardly in terms of the arousal of that feeling. However, the feelings aroused "directly" by music are not stabs of pain or feelings of unrequited passion, but more "primitive" feelings of tension, relaxation, surprise, and so on. These feelings do, therefore, in a sense have an "etiolated" cognitive content, in the way that Levinson specifies in "Music and Negative Emotions," but it is not an etiolated, imaginary version of an emotion which normally has a complex cognitive content (such as unrequited passion), but rather a feeling such as surprise, which by its nature just has—or can have—a relatively simple cognitive content. . . .

Now, something that most philosophical theorists of musical expression have either ignored or underemphasized is the fact that the musical expression of complex emotions is not a function of a few isolated measures here and there, as in Kivy's examples in *The Corded Shell;* rather it is very often a function of the large-scale formal structures of the piece as a whole. We cannot understand the expression of complex emotions in music apart from the continuous development of the music itself. None of the philosophical writers I have discussed has fully appreciated this point. . . .

In his celebrated book, *Emotion and Meaning in Music,* Leonard Meyer showed how the formal structure of works in the Classical and Romantic styles could be analyzed in terms of the emotional *responses* of the practiced listener: his was a kind of "Reader-Response" or rather "Listener-Response" theory of musical structure. In order to understand a piece of music, on this view, the listener has to have her feelings aroused in a certain way. If we are experienced in the style of the piece, then we have certain expectations about the way the music will develop; in a meaningful piece of music these expectations will be either frustrated or satisfied in unexpected ways. As we listen new expectations are constantly being aroused and we are just as constantly being *surprised* by novel developments, *relieved* by delayed resolutions, made *tense* by the delays, etc., etc. In short, understanding musical structure, according to Meyer, is not just a matter of detached analysis; rather, it is impossible without the arousal of feeling in the listener. . . .

If a piece of music is heard as successively disturbing and reassuring, or as meandering uncertainly before moving forward confidently, or as full of obstacles which are with difficulty overcome, this is at least in part because of the way the music makes us feel. Disturbing passages disturb us; reassuring ones reassure. Passages that meander uncertainly make us feel uneasy: it is not clear where the music is going. Passages that move forward confidently make us feel satisfied: we know what is happening and seem to be able to predict what will happen next. Passages that are full of obstacles make us feel tense and when the obstacles are overcome, we feel relieved. It is important to notice that the feeling *expressed* is not always the feeling *aroused:* an uncertain, diffident passage may make me uneasy; a confident passage may make me feel reassured or relaxed.

Now, of course we are still a long way from showing how unrequited passion can be expressed by a piece of music, but we can perhaps begin to see how the development of a complex piece of music can mirror the development of a complex emotional experience, and how we can become aware of both the formal development and the corresponding emotional development by means of the relatively "simple" feelings that are *aroused* in the listener as she follows that development. As I listen to a piece which expresses serenity tinged with doubt, I myself do not have to feel serenity tinged with doubt, but the feelings I do experience, such as relaxation or reassurance, interspersed with uneasiness, alert me to the nature of the overall emotional expressiveness in the piece of music as a whole. Consider, for example, a piece of music in sonata form in which the two chief themes in their initial formulation are respectively lively and ponderous (we can suppose that the contour theory accounts for these characterizations). Now, suppose that the initially lively theme (in the major) gets gradually but relentlessly overwhelmed by the ponderous (minor) theme in such a way that the first theme is never allowed to return to its initial lively formulation but gets increasingly distorted, becomes darker and is finally heard in a truncated form in the same minor key as the ponderous theme. Such music might well make me feel increasingly nervous and tense, even disturbed, as it develops. On the view I am suggesting, the emotional experience aroused by the music is essential to the detection of the emotional expressiveness in the music itself. At the same time, the emotions aroused in me are not the emotions expressed by the music. *I* feel nervous, tense, and disturbed; the *music* expresses cheerful confidence turned to despair, or something of this sort. If this account is correct, then it shows that Kivy is wrong to suppose that expressiveness in music is just a matter of contour and convention, even if some expressive passages in music can be explained in such terms. In my example, it is not enough to spot the respective lively and ponderous contours of the initial statements of the two themes; the expressiveness of the piece as a whole can only be grasped if the listener's feelings are aroused in such a way that they provide a clue to both the formal and the expressive structure of the piece as it develops through time. . . .

Representation in Music

Roger Scruton

Music may be used to express emotion, to heighten a drama, to emphasize the meaning of a ceremony; but it is nevertheless an abstract art, with no power to represent the world. Representation, as I understand it, is a property that does not belong to music.

The word 'representation' has many uses, and may often be applied to music. Therefore I shall discuss not the word, but the phenomenon, as it occurs in poetry, drama, sculpture and painting. Being common to both painting and poetry, this phenomenon cannot be identified with the semantic properties of a linguistic system, for painting, unlike poetry, does not belong to such a system. How, then, is it to be characterized? I suggest the following five conditions, not as an analysis, but as a partial description of the aesthetic significance of representation:

An excerpt

1 A man understands a representational work of art only if he gains *some* awareness of what it represents. His awareness may be incomplete, but is must be adequate. He may not see Masaccio's *Tributute Money* as a representation of the scene from the Gospel; but to understand it as a representation he should at least see the fresco as a group of gesturing men. If a man does not see the fresco in some such way—say because he can appreciate it only as an abstract arrangement of colours and lines—then he does not understand it.

2 Representation requires a medium, and is understood only when the distinction between subject and medium has been recognized. Merely to *mistake* a painting for its subject is to misunderstand it; so too is there misunderstanding when a man is unable to extract the features of the subject from the peculiarities and conventions of the medium. (A varnished painting of a man is not a painting of a varnished man, however much it may look as though it were.)

3 Interest in a representation requires an interest in its subject. If an interest in the Masaccio depends in no way upon an interest in the scene portrayed, then the fresco is being treated not as a representation but as a work of abstract art.

4 A representational work of art must express thoughts about its subject, and an interest in the work should involve an understanding of those thoughts. (This is an ingredient in condition 3.) I mean by 'thought' roughly what Frege meant by '*Gedanke*': the sense or content of a declarative sentence. In this sense thoughts may be spoken of as true or false, although of course it is not always the truth-value of a thought that is of interest in aesthetic understanding. It is clear that a representational work of art always conveys thoughts, in this Fregean sense, about its subject. Among the thoughts that give rise to my interest in *King Lear,* and which give a reason for that interest, are thoughts about Lear. These thoughts are communicated by the play, and are common property among all who understand it. Something similar occurs in the appreciation of a painting. Even in the most minimal depiction—say, of an apple on a cloth—appreciation depends on determinate thoughts that could be expressed in language without reference to the picture; for example: 'Here is an apple; the apple rests on a cloth; the cloth is chequered and folded at the edge.' Representation, in other words, is essentially propositional.

Sometimes we feel that a work of art is filled with thought, but that the thought cannot be detached from the work. It is impossible to put it into words (or into other words). Such cases, I should like to say, are cases not of representation but of expression. Why I should make such a distinction, and why I should make it in that way, will be apparent later.

5 Interest in representation may involve an interest in its *lifelike* quality; but it is not, for all that, an interest in literal truth. It is irrelevant that the depiction be inaccurate; what matters is that it be convincing. To require accuracy is to ask for a report rather than a representation.

I shall rely on an intuitive understanding of these conditions: they tell us what it is to treat something as a representation, rather than as a report, a copy, or a mere inarticulate sign. On this account, what makes a passage of prose into a representation is not so much its semantic structure as the specific intention with which it is composed.

The semantic structure is relevant only because it provides the means whereby that intention is fulfilled. Representational literature is literature written with the intention that conditions 1–5 should be satisfied. Thus one may treat as a representation something that is not a representation; one may achieve representation by novel means; one may create a representation that is never understood, and so on.

Now some philosophers—those who think that music is a language—will give an account of musical representation on the model of description in prose or verse. But such an approach is surely most implausible. Anything that we could envisage as a semantic interpretation of music (a theory of 'musical truth') would deprive music of precisely the aesthetic aims for which we admire it, turning it instead into a clumsy code. Furthermore, all attempts to explain music in such terms end by giving rules of reference without rules of truth. We are told that a certain passage carries a reference to love; but we are not told what the passage is supposed to *say* about love. And to speak of language where there is 'reference,' but no predication, is simply to misuse a word. We are in fact leaving the realm of representation altogether and entering into that of expression. But there is no need to prove that music is a language in order to assign to it the expressive properties that are mentioned, for example, by Deryck Cooke.

A better attempt to prove that music is a representational medium begins by comparing music to painting. It can be said with some truth that music, like painting, may deliberately 'imitate,' or 'copy' features of an object. Is this not, then, a kind of representation? Examples are familiar: Saint-Saëns' *Carnaval des Animaux,* 'Gretchen am Spinnrade,' *La Mer.* And it is natural to consider such pieces as attempts to 'depict' the objects referred to in their titles. But perhaps what is meant here by 'depiction' is not what is meant when we refer to the visual arts. A few observations about painting will therefore be appropriate.

It is a commonplace that depiction is not simply a matter of resemblance. Nor is it enough that the resemblance be *intended;* nor even that the artist should intend the resemblance to be noticed. No doubt Manet intended us to notice the resemblance between his *Olympia* and Titian's *Venus of Urbino.* But that is certainly not a case of one painting representing another. It is for such reasons that we might wish to lay the burden of our analysis of depiction on the notion of an 'aspect.' The artist intends that the spectator should *see* the painting *as* its subject, not merely that the spectator should notice a resemblance between the two. In other words, the painter intends that we should have the experience of a certain aspect—that we should feel that seeing his painting is importantly *like* seeing its subject—and not merely that we should notice a resemblance. Thus a painter may intend to copy the *Mona Lisa,* but he does not (as a rule) intend that his painting should be seen as Leonardo's; rather, he intends that it should be seen as the woman in Leonardo's painting. On this view, the intention in depicting is not to 'copy' an object, but rather to create a certain visual impression. And surely, it will be argued, precisely the same process, and the same intention, may exist in writing music. Sounds are created which are meant to be *heard as* other things, as the babbling of brooks, the warbling of birds, the roaring and plodding of animals. . . .

However, a difficulty now arises. . . .

Representation can be begun . . . only where it can also be completed. If music is to be representational, then its subject must be not only picked out, but also characterized. But that requires a context, and in music the context seems to add no further precision to the 'representational' parts. A certain passage in *Der Rosenkavalier* 'imitates' the glitter of a silver rose. But what more does this passage say about the glitter, except that it is a glitter (and even that may go unnoticed)? The context adds nothing to the thought, and while there is *musical* development, the development of a *description* seems scarcely to be in point. So too, when the imitation of birdsong in Messiaen is given musical development, there is no thought about the birdsong which is made more determinate by that process. The birdsong is absorbed into the musical structure and takes on a meaning that is purely musical. But, it might be said, does not the music none the less convey a thought about the birdsong, in the sense of a purely *musical* thought? Why should it matter that the thought cannot be put into words? Such a retort gets us nowhere. For whatever is meant by a purely musical thought, we can envisage also a purely painterly thought—a thought that finds its only expression in lines and colours, but which cannot be put into words, and which consequently cannot be regarded as true or false. And it is part of the point of calling painting a representational art that the thoughts involved in its appreciation are *not* all purely painterly, that, on the contrary, an experience of a painting will involve thoughts about its subject, thoughts that could be put into words. This 'narrative' element is an essential feature of the phenomenon of representation. If we insist none the less that there is a type of 'representation' that is purely symbolic (which contains ostension but no description) then we are simply denying the role of representation in aesthetic interest.

It is true, all the same, that I may hear a passage of music as something that I know it not to be. I may hear a passage as forest murmurs, for example, as rushing water, as an approaching or receding horse. Should we lay any emphasis on this phenomenon? One problem is that a man may hear and appreciate 'representational' music *without* hearing the aspect. And while it is true that I may also hear poetry without knowing what it says (as when I listen to the reading of a poem in Chinese), to do so is not to appreciate the poem as poetry. An interest in poetry is not an interest in pure sound; a genuine interest in music, on the other hand, may by-pass its representational pretensions altogether. Therefore we cannot assume that a composer may sit down with the honest intention of creating a piece to be heard as, say, the quarrel between Mr Pickwick and Mrs Bardell's lawyers. For he cannot be sure that it *will* be heard in that way; his intention is vitiated, and must be replaced by what is at best a hope or a wish. If the intention endures none the less, it is because there is available to the composer some independent way of specifying his subject: for instance, through the words of a song, or through action on the stage. Thus, in the more adventurous attempts at representation, such as we find in the symphonic poem, the composer is apt to depend on a specific literary reference in order to secure the hearer's complicity in what is better described as an imaginative endeavour than as an inevitable perception. It is thus with *Don Juan* and *Don Quixote,* with *Taras Bulba* and the anecdotal works of Charles Ives.

The argument is of course by no means conclusive. But certain facts are significant all the same. It is significant, for example, that, while a man may look at an untitled picture and know immediately what it represents, it is most unlikely that he should do the same with an untitled symphonic poem. Significant too is the indefiniteness of the relation between music and its 'subject': the music does not determine some one natural class of interpretations, and can usually be fitted to widely contrasting themes. A quarrel between Mr Pickwick and a lawyer may be 'represented' by music that serves equally well the purpose of 'depicting' a forest fire. We see this ambiguity evidenced in the ballet, where the action is usually left so far indeterminate by the music that several incompatible choreographies may exist side by side as accepted members of the repertoire; as in *The Rite of Spring.* Hence, while the aspect of a painting, and the meaning of a sentence, are publicly recognized facts, which make possible the intention characteristic of representational art, there are no similar facts to enable the intention to be carried over into the realm of music. . . .

When we learn of a piece of music that it *is* supposed to represent something, then its 'auditory aspect' (the way it sounds) may change for us, even when what is 'depicted' is not a sound. On learning of its subject we may come to 'hear it differently,' despite the fact that the subject is not something audible. Consider Debussy's prelude, *Voiles,* which may be said to depict the slow drift of sails in a summer breeze. Learning that, I may begin to hear in the musical line a leisurely and day-dreaming quality that I did not hear before, as though I were watching the to-ing and fro-ing of sails on a calm bright sea. But here, of course, what is 'depicted' is not something heard. May we not say, all the same, that we *hear* the music *as* the drifting of sails?

Even if we grant the force of those remarks, however, we find ourselves facing another, and yet more serious objection to the view that there is 'representation' in music. The objection is that one can understand a 'representational' piece of music without treating it as a representation, indeed, without being aware that it is supposed to have such a status. On the other hand, the very suggestion that one might understand—say—Raphael's *St George* (National Gallery of Art, Washington) while being indifferent to, or ignorant of, its representational quality, is absurd. To suggest such a thing is to suggest treating the Raphael as a work of abstract art; it is to ignore the feature of representation altogether, because it is thought to be insignificant, or because it is thought to play no part in aesthetic interest. But to take such a view is simply to dismiss the problem. If I recognize the existence of a problem about music it is partly because I think that there *is* an aesthetically significant notion of representation employed in the discussion and enjoyment of painting.

Now someone might object to the view that one cannot both understand the Raphael and also have no knowledge of its subject. He might claim that at least a *partial* understanding of the painting could be achieved by studying it as a piece of abstract art. One may understand the composition of the painting, he will say, the balance of tensions between ascending and descending lines, the sequence of spatial planes, and so on, and in none of this need one have an awareness of the subject. But such a reply is wholly misguided. For it seems to suggest that these important aesthetic properties of the Raphael—composition, balance, spatial rhythm—are quite independent of the representation; whereas that is clearly not so. For example we perceive the balance between the upward thrust of the horse's hind legs and the downward pressure of the lance only because we see the two lines as filled with the forces of the things depicted—of the horse's muscles and the horseman's lance. Take away the representation and the balance too would dissolve. And the same goes for the composition. Alter the representational meaning of the horse (close its eye, for example, or attach a bangle to its hoof) and the composition would be utterly destroyed. Nothing here is comprehensible until the representation is grasped.

Let us return, then, to our example. When a passage from *Voiles* reminds me of drifting sails I do indeed hear an aspect of the music. But the *important* part of this aspect—the part that seems essential to a full musical understanding—can be perceived by someone who is deaf to the 'representation.' It is possible to hear the relaxed and leisurely quality of the musical line while being unaware that it depicts the movement of sails. The 'reference' to sails does not determine our understanding of the music in the way that representation determines our understanding of the visual arts. . . .

In search for examples of genuine musical representation we may be led by this argument back to the suggestion that the true subject-matter of music is sound. Sounds have properties which music, being itself sound, may share; so music ought to be able to depict *sounds.* For there will be no difficulty here in explaining how it is that the music may lead us *inevitably* to the thought of what is represented. Thoughts of a subject will therefore form an integral part of musical appreciation. But again there is a peculiarity that deserves mention, since it seems to suggest that even here, in the most plausible examples, there is yet another of our five features of understanding representation that fails to belong to music: feature 2. When music attempts the direct 'representation' of sounds it has a tendency to become transparent, as it were, to its subject. Representation gives way to reproduction, and the musical medium drops out of consideration altogether as superfluous. In a sense the first scene of *Die Meistersinger* contains an excellent representation of a Lutheran chorale. But then it *is* a Lutheran chorale. Similarly, the tinkling of teaspoons in Strauss's *Sinfonia Domestica,* and the striking of anvils in *Rheingold,* are not so much sounds represented as sounds reproduced, which in consequence detach themselves from the musical structure and stand out on their own. Nor is this an accident. On the contrary, it is an inevitable consequence of the logical properties of sounds. For sounds . . . may be identified as individuals independently of the objects that possess them. In attempting to represent them, therefore, one need have no regard to the object that produces them: one represents the sound alone. But since there is nothing to music except sound, there ceases to be any *essential* difference between the medium of representation and the subject represented. . . .

Beneath Interpretation

Richard Shusterman

Since our current hermeneutic turn derives in large part from the rejection of foundationalism, it is not surprising that the central arguments for hermeneutic universalism* turn on rejecting foundationalist ideas of transparent fact, absolute and univocal truth, and mind-independent objectivity. For such ideas underwrite the possibility of attaining some perfect God's-eye grasp of things as they really are, independent of how we differently perceive them, a seeing or understanding that is free from the corrigibility and perspectival pluralities and prejudices that we willingly recognize as intrinsic to all interpretation.

I think the universalists are right to reject such foundational understanding, but wrong to conclude from this that all understanding is interpretation. Their mistake, a grave but simple one, is to equate the nonfoundational with the interpretive. In other words, what the universalists are successfully arguing is that all understanding is non-foundational; that it is always corrigible, perspectival, and somehow prejudiced or prestructured; that no meaningful experience is passively neutral and disinterestedly non-selective. But since, in the traditional foundationalist framework, interpretation is contrasted and designated as *the* form of non-foundational understanding, the inferior foster home of all corrigible, perspectival perception, it is easy to confuse the view that no understanding is foundational with the view that all understanding is interpretive. Yet this confusion of hermeneutic universalism betrays an unseemly residual bond to the foundationalist framework, in the assumption that what is not foundational must be interpretive. It thus prevents the holists from adopting a more liberating pragmatist perspective which (I shall argue) can profitably distinguish between understanding and interpretation without thereby endorsing foundationalism. Such pragmatism more radically recognizes uninterpreted realities, experiences, and understandings as already perspectival, prejudiced, and corrigible—in short, as non-foundationally given.

So much for a general overview of the universalist arguments. I now want to itemize and consider six of them in detail. Though there is some overlap, we can roughly divide them into three groups, respectively based on three ineliminable features of all understanding: (a) corrigibility, (b) perspectival plurality and prejudice, and (c) mental activity and process.

An excerpt

*Hermeneutic universalism is the view that all human experience is the product of interpretation.—eds.

(1) What we understand, what we grasp as truth or fact, frequently turns out to be wrong, to require correction, revision, and replacement by a different understanding. Moreover, this new understanding is typically achieved by reinterpreting the former understanding and can itself be replaced and shown to be not fact but "mere interpretation" by a subsequent understanding reached through interpretive thought. Since any putative fact or true understanding can be revised or replaced by interpretation, it cannot enjoy an epistemological status higher than interpretation; and interpretation is paradigmatically corrigible and inexhaustive. This is sometimes what is meant by the claim that there are no facts or truths but only interpretations.

The inference, then, is that since understanding is epistemologically no better than interpretation, it is altogether no different from interpretation (as if all meaningful differences had to be differences of apodicticness!). The conclusion is reinforced by the further inference that since all interpretation is corrigible and all understanding is corrigible, then all understanding is interpretation. Once formulated, the inferences are obviously (indeed pathetically) fallacious. But we tend to accept their conclusion, since we assimilate all corrigible and partial understanding to interpretation, as if genuine understanding itself could never be revised or enlarged, as if understanding had to be interpretive to be corrigible. But why make this rigidly demanding assumption? Traditionally, the reason was that understanding (like its cognates truth and fact) was itself defined in contrast to "mere interpretation" as that which *is* incorrigible. But if we abandon foundationalism by denying that any understanding is incorrigible, the idea of corrigible understanding becomes possible and indeed necessary; and once we recognize this idea, there is no need to infer that all understanding must be interpretation simply because it is corrigible. When hermeneutic universalists make this inference, they show an unintended and unbecoming reliance on the foundationalist linkage of uninterpreted understanding with incorrigible, foundational truth.

(2) The second argument for hermeneutic universalism derives from understanding's ineliminable perspectival character and the plurality of perspectives. . . . [Alexander] Nehamas builds . . . [an] argument that all understanding is interpretive on the premise that all understanding, indeed "all our activity is partial and perspectival." I think the premise is perfectly acceptable and can be established by an argument which Nehamas does not supply. All understanding must be perspectival or aspectual, since all thought and perception exhibit intentionality (in the phenomenological sense of being about something) and all intentionality is aspectual, i.e., grasping its object in a certain way. But the very idea of perspective or aspect implies that there are other possible perspectives or aspects which lie (in Gadamer's words) outside "the horizon" of a particular perspectival standpoint and thus outside its "range of vision." . . . Thus there can be no univocal and exclusive understanding of any thing, but rather many partial or perspectival ways of seeing it, none of which provides total and exclusive truth.

So much for the premise; but how does it follow that all understanding is interpretive? Again, in the traditional foundationalist framework, interpretation marks the realm of partial, perspectival, and plural ways of human understanding in essential contrast to some ideal understanding that grasps things as they really are univocally, exhaustively, and absolutely. Rejecting the very possibility and intelligibility of such univocal and complete understanding (as Nehamas and Gadamer rightly do), the universalists infer that all understanding is thereby reduced to interpretation—the foundationalist category for understanding which is not necessarily false or illegitimate (not a *mis*understanding) but which cannot represent true understanding since it is perspectivally plural and not necessarily and wholly true. However, again we should realize that once we are free of foundationalism's doctrines, there is no need to accept its categorizations. There is thus no need to deny that true understanding can itself be perspectivally partial and plural, and consequently no reason to conclude that since all understanding must be perspectival, it must also be interpretation.

(3) In speaking of understanding as perspectival and hence partial, we have so far meant that it cannot exclude different perspectives and can in principle always be supplemented. But partiality also has the central sense of bias and prejudice. The third argument why understanding must always be interpretation is that it is always prejudiced and never neutrally transparent. This is a key point in the Nietzschean, Gadamerian, and even pragmatist attacks on foundationalist understanding. Any understanding involves the human element which prestructures understanding in terms (and in service) of our interests, drives, and needs, which significantly overlap but also frequently diverge among different societies and individuals. Moreover, for Nietzsche, Gadamer, and the pragmatists, the fact that understanding is always motivated and prejudiced by our needs and values is a very good thing; it is what allows us to thrive and survive so that we can understand anything at all.

From the premise that "all understanding inevitably involves some prejudice," . . . "that every view depends on and manifests specific values" and "antecedent commitments," . . . it is but a short step to the view that all understanding and perception is interpretation. But it is a step where the more canny pragmatist fears to tread, and where she parts company from grand continental hermeneuts like Nietzsche and Gadamer. In rejecting the foundationalist idea and ideal of transparent mirroring perception, she recognizes that understanding is always motivated and prejudiced, just like interpretation. But she wonders why this makes understanding always interpretive. It just does not follow, unless we presume that *only* interpretation could be prejudiced, while (preinterpretive) understanding or experience simply could not be. But to her, this inference is as strange and offensive as a sexist argument that all humans are really women because they all are influenced by emotions, while presumably real men are not.

(4) The fourth argument for hermeneutic universalism inhabits the overlap between understanding's perspectival partiality and its active process. The argument is basically that since all understanding is selective—focused on some things and features but not on others—all understanding must therefore be interpretive. The fact that understanding is perspectivally partial (in both senses of incompleteness and purposive bias) implies that it is always selective. It always grasps some things rather than others, and what it grasps depends in part on its antecedent purposes.

This much seems uncontestable. What I challenge is the inference that since understanding (or indeed any intelligent activity) is always selective, it is therefore always interpretive. Such a conclusion needs the further premise that all purposive selection must be the product of interpretive thinking and decision. But this premise is false, an instance of the philosophical fallacy Dewey dubbed "intellectualism." For most of the selection involved in our ordinary acts of perception and understanding is done automatically and unconsciously (yet still intelligently and not mechanically) on the basis of intelligent habits, without any reflection or deliberation at all. Interpretation, in its standard ordinary usage, certainly implies conscious thought and deliberate reflection; but not all intelligent and purposive selection is conscious or deliberate. Walking down the stairs requires selecting how and where to place one's feet and body; but such selection involves interpreting only in cases of abnormal conditions when descent of the staircase presents a problem (as with an unusually dark or narrow winding staircase, a sprained ankle, or a fit of vertigo).

Just as it is wrong to confuse all purposive intelligent choice with interpretive decisions requiring ratiocination, so we can distinguish perceptions and understandings that are immediately given to us (albeit only corrigibly and based on prior experience) from understandings reached only by interpretive deliberation on the meaning of what is immediately given. When I awake on the beach at Santa Cruz with my eyes pierced by sunlight, I immediately perceive or understand it is daytime; only when I instead wake to a darkish gloom do I need to interpret that it is no longer night but merely another dreary morning in Philadelphia.

In short, I am arguing that although all understanding is selective, not all selective understanding is interpretive. If understanding's selection is neither conscious nor deliberate but prereflective and immediate, we have no reason to regard that selection or the resultant understanding as interpretation, since interpretation standardly implies some deliberate or at least conscious thinking, whereas understanding does not. We can understand something without thinking about it at all; but to interpret something we need to think about it. This distinction may recall a conclusion from Wittgenstein's famous discussion of seeing-as, where he distinguishes seeing from interpreting: "To interpret is to think, to do something; seeing is a state."

(5) Though insightful, Wittgenstein's remark is also problematic. For it suspiciously suggests that we could see or understand without doing anything; and this suspicion suggests the fifth argument for hermeneutic universalism. Understanding or perceiving, as Nietzscheans, pragmatists, and even Gadamerians insist, is active. It is not a passive mirroring, but an active structuring of what is encountered. To hear or see anything, before we even attempt to interpret it, involves the activity of our bodies, certain motor responses and tensions in the muscles and nerves of our organs of sensation. To characterize seeing or understanding in sharp contrast to interpretation as an achieved "state" rather than as "doing something" suggests that understanding is static rather than active; and if passively static, then it should be neutral rather than selective and structuring. The fifth argument for hermeneutic universalism therefore rejects this distinction between understanding as passively neutral and interpretation as actively structuring, and then infers that since all understanding is active, all understanding must be interpretive.

My response to this argument should already be clear. As a pragmatist, I fully accept the premise that all perception and understanding involve doing something;

but I deny this entails that they always involve interpretation. The inference relies on an implicit premise that all "doings" that are cognitively valuable or significant for thought are themselves already cases of thinking. Hence any active selection and structuring of perception must already be a thoughtful, deliberate selection, one involving an interpretive decision. This is the premise I contest, the assimilating conflation of all active, selective, and structuring intelligence with the active, selective structuring of the interpreting intellect. Understanding can actively structure and select without engaging in interpretation, just as action can be intelligent without engaging thought or the intellect. When, on my way to the beach, I am told that the surf is up, I immediately understand what is said, prereflectively selecting and structuring the sounds and meanings I respond to. I do not need to interpret what is said or meant. Only if I were unfamiliar with idiomatic English, or unable to hear the words, or in a situation where the utterance seemed out of place, would I have to interpret it. Only if there were some problem in understanding, some puzzle or doubt or incongruity, would I have to thematize the utterance as something that needed interpretation, something to think about and clarify or resolve.

(6) But this assertion is precisely what is challenged by the sixth argument for universal hermeneutics, an argument which highlights the intimate link between the hermeneutic turn and the linguistic turn in both continental and Anglo-American philosophy. Briefly and roughly, the argument goes as follows. All understanding is linguistic, because all understanding (as indeed all experience) involves concepts that require language. But linguistic understanding is essentially a matter of decoding or interpreting signs which are arbitrary rather than natural and whose translation into meaningful propositions thus requires interpretation. To understand the meaning of a sentence, we need, on the Quinean-Davidsonian model, to supply a translation or interpretation of it in terms already familiar to us (whether those terms be in the interpreted language itself or in another more familiar "home" language). So Davidson boldly asserts that "All understanding of the speech of another involves radical interpretation," and firmly equates "the power of thought" with "speaking a language." And from the continental tradition, Gadamer concurs by basing the universal scope of hermeneutics on "the essential linguisticality of all human experience of the world" and on a view of language as "itself the game of interpretation that we are all engaged in every day." Hence, not only all understanding but all experience is interpretive, since both are ineliminably linguistic—a conclusion endorsed by Rorty, Derrida, and a legion of hermeneutic universalists.

Though the consensus for this position is powerful, the argument strikes me as less than persuasive. It warrants challenging on two points at least. First, we can question the idea that linguistic understanding is always the decoding, translation, or interpretation of arbitrary signs through rules of meaning and syntax. This is, I think, an overly formalistic and intellectualized picture of linguistic understanding. Certainly it is not apparent that we always (or ever) interpret, decode, or translate the uncoded and unproblematic utterances we hear in our native tongue simply in order to understand them. That is precisely why ordinary language distinguishes such direct and simple understandings from decodings, translations, and interpretations.

The hermeneutic universalists will object that we must be interpreting here, even if we don't realize it, since no other model can account for our understanding. But an alternative model *is* available in Wittgenstein, where linguistic understanding is a matter of being able to make the right responses or moves in the relevant language-game, and where such ability or language-acquisition is first gained by brute training or drill. Language mastery is (at least in part) the mastery of intelligent habits of gesture and response for engaging effectively in a form of life, rather than the mastery of a system of semiotic rules for interpreting signs.

So I think a case can be made for some distinction between understanding and interpreting language, between an unreflective but intelligent trained habit of response and a thoughtful decision about how to understand or respond. I have to interpret or translate most utterances I hear in German in order to understand them, but I understand most sentences I hear in English without interpreting them; I interpret only those that seem unclear or insufficiently understood. To defend the conflation of understanding with interpretation by arguing that in simply understanding those alleged uninterpreted utterances, I am in fact already interpreting sounds as words—or, perhaps further, that my nervous system is busy interpreting vibrations into sounds—is not only to stretch the meaning of "interpretation" for no productive purpose; it is also to misrepresent our actual experience. Certainly we can make a distinction between the words and the sounds, and between the sounds and the vibrations that cause them. But this does not mean they are really distinct or distinguishable in experience and that I must therefore interpret the sounds in order to understand them as words. On the contrary, when I hear a language I understand, I typically don't hear the sounds at all but only the understood words or message. If any interpretive effort is needed, it is to hear the words as sounds or vibrations, not vice versa.

Secondly, even if we grant that linguistic understanding is always and necessarily interpretation, it still would not follow that all understanding is interpretive. For that requires the further premise that all understanding and meaningful experience is indeed linguistic. And such a premise, though it be the deepest dogma of the linguistic turn in both analytic and continental philosophy, is neither self-evident nor immune to challenge. Certainly there seem to be forms of bodily awareness or understanding that are not linguistic in nature and that in fact defy adequate linguistic characterization, though they can be somehow referred to through language. As dancers, we understand the sense and rightness of a movement or posture proprioceptively, by feeling it in our spine and muscles, without translating it into conceptual linguistic terms. We can neither learn nor properly understand the movement simply by being talked through it. . . .

What Is Going on in a Dance?

Monroe C. Beardsley

I begin these rather tentative and exploratory reflections by calling upon some provocative remarks by George Beiswanger, from an essay written some years ago and later reprinted:

> Muscular capacity is the physical means by which dances are made. But the means become available to the choreographic imagination only through the operation of a metaphor, a metaphor by which a *moving* in the muscular sense takes on the character of a *doing* or *goings on*. . . . Strictly speaking, then, dances are not made out of but *upon* movement, movement being the poetic bearer, the persistent metaphor, by which muscular material is made available for the enhanced, meaningful, and designed *goings-on* that are dance.

Though this passage summarizes a view that I shall try to defend and articulate, the attempt to apply the concept of metaphor troubles me: it seems a strained extension of an otherwise reasonably clear and useful term. So instead of Beiswanger's rather mysterious "operation of a metaphor," I shall suggest that we employ some concepts and principles borrowed from the philosophical theory of action. But I still like his favored expression for what we are all trying to understand better—those special "goings-on" that constitute dance.

A partial, though basic, description of what is going on would be to say, using terms provided by Beiswanger (but I am also borrowing language from legal theorists such as John Austin and Oliver Wendell Holmes), that there are willed muscular contractions that cause changes of position in human bodies or parts of bodies. Such caused changes we may agree to call "bodily motions," or simply *motions,* assuming them to be—with surely few exceptions—voluntary. (For even if push comes to shove in a certain symbolic sense, I take it that no one is actually knocked off balance. But for a dancer to be lifted up or carried from one location to another is not a motion, in my sense, of that dancer, though it requires motions by other dancers.)

Bodily motions are actions; they are, in one sense, basic actions, the foundation of all other actions, at least as far as we are concerned today; for even if there are such things as purely *mental* actions, in which no muscle is disturbed, these cannot be the stuff or raw material of dance. But as Beiswanger says, bodily motions are not themselves the goings-on we label *Afternoon of a Faun* or *Jewels.* It is actions of another sort that we witness and wonder at; how, then, are these related to bodily motions?

An excerpt

An extremely fruitful discovery of philosophical action theory is that actions build upon, or grow out of, each other in certain definable ways. The wielding of a hammer, say, can become, in capable hands, the driving of a nail, and that in turn a step in the building of a house. One action, in a technical sense, is said to "generate" another action that is its fruition or even its aim. Thus we can analyze and come to understand certain actions by examining their *generating conditions*—that is, the conditions that are to be fulfilled in order for act A to generate act B. This is easy in some cases; clearly it is the presence of the nail and the wood, in proper relationship, that converts the swinging of a hammer into the driving of a nail and that enables the former action to generate the latter action: *in* or *by* swinging the hammer, the carpenter drove the nail. Now there is, of course, an endless variety of such sets of generating conditions; however, they fortunately fall into a limited number of classes, and these classes themselves belong to two fundamental categories. The first is *causal generation.* Since the swinging of the hammer *causes* the nail to penetrate the two-by-four studding, the swinging of the hammer *generates* the (act of) driving the nail into the wood. If the hammer misses or the nail is balked by a knot, this act-generation does not occur.

In this first category of act-generation, one action generates a second action that is numerically distinct from it: swinging the hammer is not the same action as driving the nail (or building the house). In the second category, no new action, yet a different kind of action, is generated. If a person mistakenly believes that his or her divorce is final and legal and so marries a second spouse, that person has (unintentionally) committed bigamy; given the generating conditions (the persisting legal bond), the act of marrying generates the act of committing bigamy. The person has not done two things, but two kinds of things: the same action was both an act of marrying and an act of bigamy. This I call *sortal generation:* the act-generation that occurs when an action of one sort becomes also (under the requisite conditions) an action of another sort—without, of course, ceasing to be an action of the first sort as well.

These concepts, simple as they are, can help us clarify idioms sometimes used by dance theorists. Thus when George Beiswanger says that "dances are not made out of but *upon* movement" (and remember he is using the term *movement* the way I am using the term *motion*), we can interpret him, I think, as saying that a dance is not composed of, does not have as its parts or elements, bodily motions, but rather is in some way sortally generated by those motions: under certain conditions, the motion "takes on the character" (as he says) of a dance-movement. And if I may be permitted the license, I should like to take advantage of the dancer's cherished special use of the word *moving* and use it in a nominative form to refer to *actions that have the character of a dance:* I shall call them *movings.* Thus when Beiswanger adds, "Dance does consist of *goings-on* in the act of coming to be," I shall adopt a somewhat more cautious paraphrase: *in a dance, movings are sortally generated by bodily motions.* And this proposition must be supplemented at once to forestall an imminent objection: certainly there are rests in dance as well as doings, and these, however passive, are part and parcel of what is happening (it happens for a time that nothing happens). Muscular contractions may be needed to maintain a position as well as to change one—especially if it is to stand on tiptoe with arm and leg outstretched. So, besides motions we shall have to include *bodily pauses* or cessations of motion; and we can add that just as motions can generate movings, so pauses can generate *posings* (using this term for peculiarly dance states of affairs). Thus we may now propose the following: *dancing is sortally generating movings by bodily motions and posings by bodily pauses.*

Thus I find myself in disagreement—not wholly verbal, I think—with a recent valuable essay by Haig Khatchadourian. It has been effectively criticized on several points by Julie Van Camp, and I shall not review her objections here but only call attention to a few other matters. According to Khatchadourian, "Dancing consists of movements and not, or not also, of actions of some kind or other." First, although this distinction—which I hope to clarify shortly—may seem oversubtle, I believe (with Beiswanger) that dancing consists not in what Khatchadourian calls movements—that is, motions—but in actions generated by them. And second, I think it is a mistake—and there seems no warrant for this in action theory—to divide bodily motions from actions: they *are* actions of a certain kind, though in themselves generally not as interesting as the actions they generate. However, Khatchadourian's distinction between (as I would say) bodily motions and *other* actions is important; but then the distinguishing features of these other actions need to be spelled out.

Taking off from the first of these two objections to Khatchadourian, I must now try to explain why I say that movings are more than motions: that there is indeed act-generation, a transformation of motions into movings. I have two main reasons.

My first reason rests on two propositions that will probably not be challenged. (1) It seems we do not dance all of the time—not every motion is dancing—so there must be some difference between the motions that generate dancing and those that don't, however difficult it may be to get a fix on. (2) It seems there is nothing in the nature of motions themselves that marks off those that can be dance from those that can't; practically any kind is available. Some insight into the puzzles here may be derived from Marcia Siegel's discussion of Anna Sokolow's *Rooms.* She describes the various motions of the performers—for example,

> Then, drooping across the chair seats, they lower their heads to the floor, lift their arms to the side and let them drop, slapping against the floor with a dead sound. . . . Slowly they lean forward and back in their seats, staring at the audience.
>
> None of this can be called dance movement, but neither is it merely the prosaic activity that it seems to be at first. Sokolow gives these ordinary movements a dancelike character by exaggerating the dynamics and the timing, sometimes beyond "natural" limits. Instead of just raising or lowering a hand, someone might take a very long time to raise it, giving the gesture great importance, then drop it suddenly and heavily, as if, having made all that effort to prepare, there was nothing worth doing with the hand after all. Besides the intensified way everything is carried out, each move or repeated series of moves is a separate gesture that finishes in some way before the next series is undertaken.

I am not sure I fully understand this passage, which is not as clear as Siegel's writing usually is. When she says that "none of this can be called dance movement," she is apparently not denying that what is going on is a dance; I think she means that these motions are not the usual stuff of dance, not conventionally used in dancing. When she adds that "Sokolow gives these ordinary movements a dancelike character," I take this to mean that Sokolow shapes the motions so that they actually *are* dance, not merely *like* dance. Of course this kind of performance is difficult to talk about, but if I understand her, Siegel is marking an important distinction. Of two motions, abstractly classified as, say, "raising an arm," one may be a dance and the other not, depending on some distinguishing feature contributed by the choreographer—so that, more concretely described, they may be somewhat different motions, though they belong to the same shared type. One motion generates moving, in my sense of the term, and the other doesn't. (Some would add that merely transferring an "ordinary" movement to a stage, under a bright spotlight, could give it a quality that makes it a dance.)

My second reason for distinguishing the concept of *motion* from that of *moving* is that this very distinction seems to be deeply embedded in a large special or technical vocabulary that is used for talking about dancing. Take the term *pirouette,* for example. We can explain "how you do" a pirouette, and we can say that in turning rapidly on her toe, the dancer pirouetted. A turning of a certain sort generated a pirouetting, and they were the same event; yet if we first describe the event as a rapid turning on the toe we are adding something to this description when we say that it was also a pirouette, for that is to say it was dancing. So with numerous other familiar terms: *jeté, glissade, demi-plié, sissone fermé, pas de bourrée.* (And, since we must not forget to include posings as well as movings, we should add *arabesque.*) My thesis is that all these terms refer to movings as such, not to the motions that generate them. When the technical terms are supplemented by other words, borrowed from ordinary speech—*leap, lope, skip, run*—these take on a second sense in the context of dance description, though I do not think this is a case of metaphor.

The question that looms next is evidently this: how does it come about that—or what are the generating conditions that make—motions and pauses become the movings and poses of dance? Without pretending to offer much of an argument, I will illustrate some features of action theory by reflecting briefly on a few possible answers to this rather large question.

First, then, let us consider an answer that is not without plausibility and is in fact suggested by Marcia Siegel. You will recall her remark that a dancer in *Rooms* "might take a very long time to raise [his or her hand], giving the gesture great importance, then drop it suddenly and heavily, as if . . . there was nothing worth doing with the hand after all." She speaks of "the intensified way everything is carried out." If we are wary, I think we can make do with the word *expressive* to mark her meaning—and mine. When I use the word in this context, I refer to *regional qualities* of a motion or sequence of motions: it has an air or momentousness or mystery or majesty; it is abrupt, loose, heavy, decisive, or languid. To say that the motion is expressive is just to say that it has some such quality to a fairly intense degree. And this is *all* I mean by "expressive." We might then try formulating our first answer in this way: *When a motion or sequence of motions is expressive, it is dance.*

Selma Jeanne Cohen, . . . apparently holds that expressiveness is present in all true dance—though her defense of this view is, I think, marred by a tendency to confuse expressiveness with other things I shall shortly touch on, such as representation and signalling. Khatchadourian, in reply, says that expressiveness is not a necessary condition of dance but a criterion of *good* dance. An objection to making it a *sufficient* condition is, for example, that an actress in a play might appropriately make exactly the same expressive motion as Sokolow's dancers yet would not be bursting into dance but dramatically revealing a mental state or trait of personality. Thus to make the first answer work we would need to introduce further restrictions on the range of regional qualities that are to be taken into account. If we look about in writings on dance, we find a diversity of terms but some convergence of meaning; take two examples from rather different quarters. As is well known, Susanne Langer speaks of "virtual powers" as the "primary illusion" of dance; and though I don't see the need for talking about illusions, I think "powers" conveys some general truth. Then there is a remark by Merce Cunningham, reported by Calvin Tomkins:

> He has remained firmly committed to dance as dance, although he acknowledges that the concept is difficult to define. "I think it has to do with amplification, with enlargement," he said recently. "Dancing provides something—an amplification of energy—that is not provided any other way, and that's what interests me."

This remark is noteworthy in part because of what it tells about Cunningham's own taste and preferences, but I think "amplification of energy" conveys a general truth.

To put my suggestion briefly, and all too vaguely: in dance the forms and characters of voluntary motion (the generating base) are encouraged to allow the emergence of new regional qualities, which in turn are lifted to a plane of marked perceptibility: they are exhibited or featured. It is the featuring specifically of the qualities of *volition,* of willing to act, that makes movings of motions. This is most obviously true when we see power, energy, force, zest, and other positive qualities of volition; but it also applies to such qualities as droopy exhaustion and mechanical compulsion—weaknesses of the will, as well as strengths. Dances of course may be expressive in other ways, have other qualities besides these volitional qualities. But the first answer to our basic question might be reformulated this way: *When a motion or sequence of motions is expressive in virtue of its fairly intense volitional qualities, it is dance. . . .*

There is also the suggestion that it is somehow the *absence* of practical intent ("no actual work in hand," he says) that distinguishes dance from other actions. This calls for another look, after we have gained a clearer notion of what "actual work" might encompass.

To get to this topic, we may take a short detour by way of another answer to our basic question, one that tries to capture an essence of dance through the concept of representation. Consider an *act-type* (that is, a kind of action, having numerous actual instances): say, snow shovelling. This involves, for effectiveness and efficiency, certain characteristic *motion-types.* If we select certain of these motion-types that distinguish snow shovelling from other activities and perform them for the benefit of someone else, we may enable the other person to recognize the action-type from which the motions have been derived. This, roughly put, is the representation (or depiction) of one action-type by an action of another type—for in representing snow shovelling, we are not actually doing it (the actor smoking a pipe onstage does not represent a man smoking a pipe, for he is one; but he may represent a detective smoking a pipe, which he is not).

Now representation by motions clearly comes in many degrees of abstraction, of which we can perhaps distinguish three degrees in a standard way. In *playacting* (as in drama) we have the most realistic degree: the actor may wield a shovel, and the director may even call for artificial snow for the actor to push about. In *miming,* we dispense with props and verbal utterance, and we allow room for witty exaggeration: the mime would be rushing about the stage, busily moving his arms in shovelling motions, stopping to blow on his fingers or to rub his aching back. In *suggesting,* we merely allude to the original action-type, borrowing a motion or two, sketching or outlining, and mingling these motions with others, such as whirling or leaping. This might be the *Snow-shovelling Dance,* to be performed, of course, after the actual job has been done, by way of celebrating the victory of humankind over one more assault of nature. Playacting, taken quite narrowly, must be comparatively rare in dance, miming much more common, though in short stretches, I should think. Suggesting, on the other hand, is pervasive; it appears in many of the most striking and cogent movings.

Indeed, it is this pervasiveness that prompts another answer to our question: *When a motion, or sequence of motions, represents actions of other types in the mode of suggestion, it is dance.* This will undoubtedly cover a lot of ground, but it will not, of course, be satisfactory to all dancers today. For beyond the third degree of abstraction in representation there lies a fourth degree, where representation disappears; we have loping-back-and-forth and panting dancers, sitting and bending dancers, who don't represent anything. Or pirouetting dancers. Now one could argue that these fragments of moving only become dance when embedded in larger sequences that do represent by suggestion. But I should think many a pas de deux as well as many a contemporary dance episode is utterly nonrepresentational.

Snow shovelling is an example of a class of actions in which we effect a change in the physical world outside our skins; it is causally generated. Many of these actions have their own characteristic, and therefore imitable, forms of motion: corn planting, baby rocking, knitting, hammering. I should like to call such actions *workings,* because they perform work in the physicist's sense—even though some of them would ordinarily be called play: kicking a field goal or sinking a putt. It is plain that dances include many representations of working actions, nearly always at a fairly high degree of abstraction. And this contributes to their expressiveness: seen as baby rocking, the motions may yield a more intense quality of gentleness.

Besides workings, we may take note of two other broad classes of action that have some bearing upon the subject of this inquiry. In one of these we are concerned, not with physical states of the world, but (indirectly) with mental states of other persons. The actions I refer to, when they are performed with the help of, or by means of, verbal utterances, are called "illocutionary actions," and they are generally of familiar types: asserting, greeting, inviting, thanking, refusing, insisting. These types have subtypes: insisting on being paid time-and-a-half for last week's overtime, for example, is a subtype that may have numerous instances. Many of these same types of action can also be performed without words; we can greet by gestures as well, or sometimes better. Nodding, shrugging, winking, bowing, kneeling might be called "para-illocutionary actions" when they are done with this sort of significance; so biting the thumb generates insulting, as in act 1, scene 2 of *Romeo and Juliet.* With or without words, such actions can be called *signallings* or *sayings,* in acknowledgment of the messages they carry. I choose the latter term, and the way to put it is: in waving a hand a certain way, the infant is saying good-bye. Sayings, like workings, are representable: in waving his or her hand, the dancer is representing someone saying good-bye. And, like working-representations, saying-representations can contribute much to the expressiveness of motions in dance. The quality of that waving, as a moving, may be intensified by its semantic aspect. The dancer summons up and draws into the texture of his or her moving something of the sorrow or finality of the action-type he or she is representing. Sayings involve a form of sortal generation, what is (very broadly) called "conventional generation." It is the existence of a social convention that enables arm waving to generate good-bying; the dancer does not make use of that convention to say anything, but recalls it to intensify expressiveness.

This raises an important question that there is no time to do more than glance at now: do dances not only represent, but also constitute sayings? That is, can motions that generate movings also generate sayings? I have read an odd remark attributed to John Cage: "We are not, in these dances, saying something. We are simple-minded enough to think that if we were saying something we would use words." This is indeed simple-minded, given the extraordinary richness of bodily motions as generators of para-illocutionary actions. It might even be argued that representations of para-illocutionary actions can hardly help but be para-illocutionary actions themselves, since by selecting the suggestive elements and giving them a different context we may seem to comment on the sayings we quote. But this claim goes beyond what I am prepared to argue for at the moment.

The third class of actions I shall call attention to consists of motions that are goal-directed, though not necessarily goal-attaining, and that have a point or purpose, even though they move neither other bodies nor other minds. Take, for example, running a race (with the aim of winning), or reaching out, or shrinking away. We might call these actions "strivings." They are generated by the presence of mental states, such as intentions (a form of "circumstantial generation"). Of course strivings, too, can be represented.

Workings, sayings, and strivings seem to belong together at some level of abstraction, as entering into social interactions that have a function, that end in achievement or are so aimed. If it is not too misleading, we may use the label "practical" for them all—and at least we will have tried to delimit the scope of this notorious weasel word somewhat more scrupulously than is usual. With its help, as so defined, we can state St. Augustine's proposal in what seems to be its most plausible form: *When a motion, or sequence of motions, does not generate practical actions, and is intended to give pleasure through perception of rhythmic order, it is dance.* But even at its best the proposal will not serve. Perhaps if we were to add a suitable insistence on expressiveness as another source of the pleasure, we would come close to an adequate characterization of dance as an art. But I assume that we do not wish to limit our concept of dance in this way. Suppose the pueblo corn dance, for example, is not only performed in order to aid the growth of corn but is actually effective; then it is a working, just as much as seed planting or hoeing. Dance shades off into and embraces some part of ritual, which is a kind of saying. If the dance is done at a festival in competition for first prize (although that may be opposed to the true spirit of dance), I suppose it is no less a dance for being at the same time a striving.

Thus we cannot define dance in this negative way as excluding motions that generate practical actions. Yet there is something to this opposition, something about dancing that is different, even if those other actions can be, in their various ways, expressive. Perhaps we can come nearer to it in one final line of thought. If *every* motion of the corn dance is prescribed in detail by magical formulas or religious rules to foster germination, growth, or a fruitful harvest, we might best regard it as pure ritual, however expressive it may be as a *consequence* of its mode of working. Like soldiers on parade or priests officiating at Mass, the participants would verge on dance but they would not really be dancing. But if some part of what goes on in the ritual helps it to achieve expressiveness (of volitional qualities) that is to some degree independent of any practical function, then whatever else it may be, it is also a moving. If, in other words, there is more zest, vigor, fluency, expansiveness, or stateliness than appears necessary for practical purposes, there is an overflow or superfluity of expressiveness to mark it as belonging to its own domain of dance.

Television and Aesthetics

Umberto Eco

. . . A popular song, a TV commercial, a comic strip, a detective novel, a Western movie were seen as more or less successful tokens of a given model or type. As such they were judged as pleasurable but non-artistic. Furthermore, this excess of pleasurability, repetition, lack of innovation, was felt as a commercial trick (the product had to meet the expectations of its audience), not as the provocative proposal of a new (and difficult to accept) world vision. The products of mass media were equated with the

An excerpt

products of industry insofar as they were produced *in series,* and the "serial" production was considered as alien to the artistic invention.

According to the modern aesthetics, the principal features of the massmedia products were repetition, iteration, obedience to a preestablished schema, and redundancy (as opposed to information).

The device of *iteration* is typical, for instance, of television commercials: one distractedly watches the playing out of a sketch, then focuses one's attention on the punch line that reappears at the end of the episode. It is precisely on this foreseen and awaited reappearance that our modest but irrefutable pleasure is based.

Likewise, the reading of a traditional detective story presumes the enjoyment of a scheme. The scheme is so important that the most famous authors have founded their fortune on its very immutability.

Furthermore, the writer plays upon a continuous series of connotations (for example, the characteristics of the detective and of his immediate "entourage") to such an extent that their reappearance in each story is an essential condition of its reading pleasure. And so we have the by now historical "tics" of Sherlock Holmes, the punctilious vanity of Hercule Poirot, the pipe and the familiar fixes of Maigret, on up to the famous idiosyncracies of the most unabashed heroes of the hard-boiled novel. Vices, gestures, habits of the character portrayed permit us to recognize an old friend. These familiar features allow us to "enter into" the event. When our favorite author writes a story in which the usual characters do not appear, we are not even aware that the fundamental scheme of the story is still like the others: we read the book with a certain detachment and are immediately prone to judge it a "minor" one. . . .

THE ERA OF REPETITION

I would like to consider now the case of an historical period (our own) for which iteration and repetition seem to dominate the whole world of artistic creativity, and in which it is difficult to distinguish between the repetition of the media and the repetition of the so-called major arts. In this period one is facing the discussion of a new theory of art, one that I would label *post-modern aesthetics,* which is revisiting the very concepts of repetition and iteration under a different profile. Recently in Italy such a debate has flourished under the standard of a "new aesthetics of seriality." I recommend my readers to take "seriality," in this case, as a very wide category or, if one wants, as another term for repetitive art.

Seriality and repetition are largely inflated concepts. The philosophy of the history of art has accustomed us to some technical meanings of these terms that it would be well to eliminate: I shall not speak of repetition in the sense of Kierkegaard, nor of "répétition différente," in the sense of Deleuze. In the history of contemporary music, series and seriality have been understood in a sense more or less opposite what we are discussing here. The dodecaphonic "series" is the opposite of the repetitive seriality typical of all the media, because there a given succession of twelve sounds is used once and only once within a single composition.

If you open a current dictionary, you will find that for "repeat" the meaning is "to say something or do something the second time or again and again; iteration of the same word, act or idea." For "series" the meaning is "a continued succession of similar things." It is a matter of establishing what it means to say "again" or "the same or similar things."

To serialize means, in some way, *to repeat.* Therefore, we shall have to define a first meaning of "to repeat" by which the term means to make a *replica* of the same *abstract type.* Two sheets of typewriter paper are both *replicas* of the same commercial *type.* In this sense one thing is the same as another when the former exhibits the same properties as the latter, at least under a certain description: two sheets of typing paper are the same from the point of view of our functional needs, even though they are not the same for a physicist interested in the molecular structure of the objects. From the point of view of industrial mass production, two "tokens" can be considered as "replicas" of the same "type" when for a normal person with normal requirements, in the absence of evident imperfection, it is irrelevant whether one chooses one instead of the other. Two copies of a film or of a book are replicas of the same type.

The repetitiveness and the seriality that interests us here look instead at something that at first glance does not appear the same as (equal to) something else.

Let us now see the case in which (1) something is offered as original and different (according to the requirements of modern aesthetics); (2) we are aware that this something is repeating something else that we already know; and (3) notwithstanding this—better, just because of it—we like it (and we buy it).

The Retake

The first type of repetition is the *retake.* In this case one recycles the characters of a previous successful story in order to exploit them, by telling what happened to them after the end of their first adventure. The most famous example of retake is Dumas's *Twenty Years Later,* the most recent ones are the "to be continued" versions of *Star Wars* or *Superman.* The retake is dependent on a commercial decision. There is no rule establishing whether the second episode of the story should reproduce, with only slight variations, the fist one, or must be a totally different story concerning the same characters. The retake is not strictly condemned to repetition. An illustrious example of retake are the many different stories of the Arthurian cycle, telling again and again the vicissitudes of Lancelot or Perceval.

The Remake

The *remake* consists in telling again a previous successful story. See the innumerable editions of *Dr. Jekyll* or of *Mutiny on the Bounty.* The history of arts and literature is full of pseudo-remakes that were able to tell at every time something different. The whole of Shakespeare is a remake of preceding stories. Therefore "interesting" remakes can escape repetition.

The Series

The *series* works upon a fixed situation and a restricted number of fixed pivotal characters, around whom the secondary and changing ones turn. The secondary characters must give the impression that the new story is different from the preceding ones, while in fact the narrative scheme does not change. . . .

To the same type belong the TV serials such as *All in the Family, Starsky and Hutch, Columbo,* etc. (I put together different TV genres that range from soap opera to situation comedy, and to the detective serial.)

With a series one believes one is enjoying the novelty of the story (which is always the same) while in fact one is enjoying it because of the recurrence of a narrative scheme that remains constant. The series in this sense responds to the infantile need of hearing again always the same story, of being consoled by the "return of the Identical," superficially disguised.

The series consoles us (the consumers) because it rewards our ability to foresee: we are happy because we discover our own ability to guess what will happen. We are satisfied because we find again what we had expected, but we do not attribute this happy result to the obviousness of the narrative structure, but to our own presumed capacities to make forecasts. We do not think, "The author has constructed the story in a way that I could guess the end," but rather, "I was so smart to guess the end in spite of the efforts the author made to deceive me."

We find a variation of the series in the structure of the flashback: we see, for example, some comic-strip stories (such as Superman) in which the character is not followed along in a straight line during the course of his life, but is continually rediscovered at different moments of his life, obsessively revisited in order to discover there new opportunities for new narratives. It seems as if these moments of his life have fled from the narrator out of absent-mindedness, but their rediscovery does not change the psychological profile of the character, which is fixed already, once and for all. In topological terms this sub-type of the series may be defined as a *loop.*

Usually the loop-series comes to be devised for commercial reasons: it is a matter of considering how to keep the series alive, of obviating the natural problem of the aging of the character. Instead of having characters put up with new adventures (that would imply their inexorable march toward death), they are made continually to relive their past. The loop solution produces paradoxes that were already the target of innumerable parodies. Characters have a little future but an enormous past, and in any case, nothing of their past will ever have to change the mythological present in which they have been presented to the reader from the beginning. Ten different lives would not suffice to make Little Orphan Annie undergo what she underwent in the first (and only) ten years of her life.

The spiral is another variation of the series. In the stories of Charlie Brown, apparently nothing happens, and any character is obsessively repeating his/her standard performance. And yet in every strip the character of Charlie Brown or Snoopy is enriched and deepened. This does not happen either with Nero Wolfe, or Starsky or Hutch: we are always interested in their new adventures, but we already know all we need to know about their psychology, their habits, their capacities, their ethical standpoints.

I would add finally that form of seriality that, in cinema and television, is motivated less by the narrative structure than by the nature of the actor himself: the mere presence of John Wayne, or of Jerry Lewis (when they are not directed by a great director, and even in these cases) succeeds in making, always, the *same* film. The author tries to invent different stories, but the public recognizes (with satisfaction) always and ever the same story, under superficial disguises. . . .

When one speaks today of the aesthetics of seriality, one alludes to something more radical, that is, to a notion of aesthetic value that wholly escapes the "modern" idea of art and literature.

It has been observed that with the phenomenon of television serials we find a new concept of "the infinity of the text"; the text takes on the rhythms of that same dailiness in which it is produced, and that it mirrors. The problem is not one of recognizing that the serial text varies indefinitely upon a basic scheme (and in this sense it can be judged from the point of view of the "modern" aesthetics). The real problem is that what is of interest is not so much the single variations as "variability"' as a formal principle, the fact that one can make variations to infinity. Variability to infinity has all the characteristics of repetition, and very little of innovation. But it is the "infinity" of the process that gives a new sense to the device of variation. What must be enjoyed—suggest the post-modern aesthetics—is the fact that a series of possible variations is potentially infinite. What becomes celebrated here is a sort of victory of life over art, with the paradoxical result that the era of electronics—instead of emphasizing the phenomena of shock, interruptions, novelty, and frustration of expectations—would produce a return to the continuum, the Cyclical, the Periodical, the Regular.

Omar Calabrese has thoroughly looked into this: from the point of view of the "modern" dialectic between repetition and innovation, one can easily recognize how in the Columbo series, for example, on a basic scheme some of the best names in American cinema have worked in variations. Thus it would be difficult to speak, in such a case, of pure repetition: if the scheme of the detection and the psychology of the protagonist actor remains unchanged, the style of the narrative changes each time. This is no small thing, especially from the point of view of the "modern" aesthetics. But it is exactly on a different idea of style that Calabrese's paper is centered. In these forms of repetition "we are not so much interested in what is repeated as we are in the way the components of the text come to be segmented and then how the segments come to be codified in order to establish a system of invariants: any component that does not belong to the system, can be defined as an *independent variable.*" In the most typical and apparently "degenerated" cases of seriality, the independent variables are not altogether the more visible, but the more microscopic, as in a homeopathic solution where the potion is all the more potent because by further "succussions" the original particles of the medicinal product have almost disappeared. This is what permits Calabrese to speak of the Columbo series as an "exercice de style" à la Queneau. We are, says Calabrese, facing a "neobaroque aesthetics" that is instantiated, not only by the "cultivated" products, but even, and above all, by those that are most degenerated. Apropos of *Dallas,* one can say that "the semantic opposition and the articulation of the elementary narrative structures can migrate in combinations of the highest improbability around the various characters."

Organized differentiations, polycentrism, regulated irregularity—such would be the fundamental aspects of this neo-baroque aesthetic, the principal example of which is musical variations à la Bach. Since in the epoch of mass communications "the condition for listening . . . as in the Kabuki theater, it may then be the most minuscule variant that will produce pleasure in the text, or that form of explicit repetition which is already known."

What results from these reflections is clear. The focus of the theoretical inquiry is displaced. Before, mass mediologists tried to save the dignity of repetition by recognizing in it the possibility of a traditional dialectic between scheme and innovation (but it was still the innovation that accounted for the value, the way of rescuing the product from degradation and promoting it to a value). Now, the emphasis must be placed on the inseparable knot of scheme-variation, where the variation is no longer more appreciable than the scheme. The term neobaroque must not deceive: we are witnessing the birth of a new aesthetic sensibility much more archaic, and truly post-postmodern.

Adorno's Case Against Popular Music

Lee B. Brown

In presenting Theodor Adorno's views on popular music, I will draw heavily upon his 1941 essay, "On Popular Music," which appeared in *Studies in Philosophy and Social Science* (Vol. IX, 1941, No. 3). I will also rely upon Adorno's general aesthetic theory, as well as some other of his writings on the entertainment industry. The examples Adorno uses in the essay are obviously dated. (His reference to "the King" is not to Elvis but to Benny Goodman.) However, if Adorno were still alive, he would almost certainly argue that very little has changed in the sphere of popular music since he wrote the piece. In this essay, I have occasionally applied his views to more recent examples.

Adorno's views about all art—high and low—are nested within a complex analysis of the history and social function of art. Unlike some philosophers, Adorno believed that art's nature changes historically. In particular, its character is altered as it becomes separated from the fabric of daily life. (To understand his point, compare modern symphonic concert music with music in its earliest forms—when it was bound up with other human activities such as birth, death, marriage, and work.) Adorno also frames his examination of the arts within a view about fundamental

---

An excerpt

changes in human rationality that he believes have taken place in the modern era. With the rise of capitalism, he maintains, things have lost touch with their original value for the sake of a secondary value, which Adorno calls *exchange value.* Put briefly, the system attempts to treat every effort of human productivity—including the arts—as commodities. If this process is not obvious to us, that is because of capitalism's ingenuity in making us accept, indeed to love, the world it has created.

One effect of modern socio-economic forces, Adorno tells us, is the development of a "purist" or "formalist" aesthetic theory. This view about art reflects the way it has learned to turn its back on ordinary life and cultivate, as best it can, an autonomous sphere unto itself. Art's use, he likes to say epigrammatically, consists in its uselessness. This hermetic impulse is art's way of resisting the invasive effects of commodification on all aspects of life; and it serves as a standard against which actual life can be measured. However, in creating its beautiful, well-organized totalities, art can all too easily become a plaything of bourgeois culture. So compromised, it tends to provide us with superficial pleasures and cheap, reassuring views of ourselves and our lives. The life of high art under capitalism is a precarious one. Meanwhile, the popular arts thrive.

The basic concepts of Adorno's analysis of popular music are the interrelated ones of *simplicity* and *standardization.* The tunes, rhythms, and harmonies of popular music, he asserts, are simple and therefore easy to comprehend. The subject matter is no less simplistic. The topics are the standard sentimental ones, for example, fantasy narratives of love in which all the real trials of life are magically resolved. Even the dark shadows in pop songs, Adorno would say, play their own fantasy roles. Consider the self-pity characteristic of so many country western songs, with their messages heroicizing human failings such as alcoholism.

Like an assembly line product, Adorno says, popular music is made of replaceable parts. To understand his point, we must bear in mind that much American popular music comes in one of two typical forms. (i) Basic rock music deriving from the *blues,* which is standardly packaged in twelve measures and moves predictably along a track built out of three chords. (ii) Most other pop songs, like "Stormy Weather," or "Shine on Harvest Moon," exhibiting the structure of Broadway show tunes. That is, they are thirty-two measures long and consist of just two tunes distributed across four eight-bar segments arranged in an AABA sequence. Such forms invite a sort of "cookie cutter" treatment. Like a washing machine or automobile with replaceable parts, if one part is "broken" or doesn't work well, another can replace it. For example, when Broadway composers found that the B section of a song was not to their liking, they would often just borrow one from another song.

Such music, Adorno believed, appeals to the infantile or "regressive" desire for repetition. Consider the hypnotic character of the well-known rhythmic pulse of most American popular music. The beat must go on . . . and on. Or consider the habit of setting a CD or record player simply to repeat a tune or album over and over again for hours on end. In psychoanalytic terms, Adorno regards such obsessive pleasures as partly masochistic—like biting your nails. The activity is partly painful, you never get full satisfaction from it, but you can't stop doing it. In different terms, one can also say that popular music offers the escapist pleasure of drugs. Like drugs, they capitalize upon the need for more of *the same.* (Consider the similarities, indeed the literal interaction, between late-century "techno" music and drugs.) The infantilism of popular music, Adorno believes, is also registered in the music's language. Lovers are typically addressed as "baby," and, indeed, the lyrics often reduce to nonsensical babbling. True, the music of "generation X" rock bands or rap groups is grittier than any popular music Adorno could have heard. But he would undoubtedly insist that current pop music recycles *its* monotonous themes over and over again just like the pop music of the past did. And he would draw attention to the way late-century pop music celebrates its cult of youth. Youth has, in effect, become a commodity.

Because of its formal and substantial simplicity, popular music offers little challenge to the mind. Adorno likes to say that the music hears *for* the listener, by which he means that it leaves no work for us to do for ourselves. This fits his view that modern listeners are deficient in real musical literacy. Consider, in this connection, that at the beginning of the present century, people were routinely taught to play the piano. Pianos have since been replaced by stereo systems. Our relationship to music is nowadays more a matter of passive consumption than of music-making.

Adorno makes a pointed comparison between a familiar example of "classical" music, Beethoven's Fifth Symphony, and a standard piece of popular music. The symphony does not consist of a few simple parts revolving repetitiously for our passive reception. First, it is complex, being made of subsidiary parts or "movements," which have subtle relationships to each other. Second, within each movement, there are significant relationships between the parts. Third, the symphony effects an elaborate transformation of its musical sources. For instance, the scherzo movement of the symphony is a form derivative from the minuet, a type of dance, which, in the Fifth, Beethoven has transmogrified almost beyond recognition. Instead of the polite tunes of a minuet, his scherzo makes use of a powerful thematic dualism, involving—in Adorno's words—a "creeping" theme in the strings contrasted with a "stone-like" response in the woodwinds. This sets up a tremendously foreboding tension, which serves, in turn, as a dramatic introduction to the triumphant music of the last movement. What might have been simple has been made complex, developmental, dramatic. The relationship between the various parts of the symphony makes demands upon our musical experience and intelligence. We are challenged to "track" what's happening. Further, one could not replace bits of the music of the Fifth with alternatives without ruining its overall sense. The placement of the bits in a piece of popular music, by contrast, is fortuitous, devoid of a "logic" of musical progression.

Adorno takes it for granted that standardization and individualization are at odds. Popular music does not speak with *anyone's* voice, anymore than a sewing machine does. However, popular music makes use of what Adorno calls *pseudo-individualization.* A good example is what is known in the industry as a "hook"—a simple chordal pattern, beat, or repeated theme, by means of which record producers try to grab us and create a hit. For example, the tune may be just different enough from others to sound special. Or, if too obviously dull, it may be embellished with superficial variations. (Consider, for example, how often a country western jukebox tune uses the rudimentary device of changing key as a way of fending off total boredom.) Some popular music—jazz, most notably—makes room for apparent individualism by means of improvisation. However, Adorno believes that such improvisation is never really the "untrammeled" thing it is touted to be. The possibilities of anything really unique happening in jazz improvisation, he says, are limited because the music is always framed within the context of a musical prison, the ongoing beat, or the overall form of the blues, for instance. As he often says, the music conveys the feeling that, in spite of its superficial individualism, you are always "on safe ground."

By such means, the industry creates music that sounds distinctive even though it really isn't. In the sixties, arguments raged about whether it was the Beatles or the Rolling Stones who *really* carried the torch of the new rock 'n' roll. The American music awards, the "Grammys," with great hoopla gives annual awards to the "best" pop groups and songs of the year. Adorno's point about such cases is that placing pop bands in competition with each other—imaginary or real—is phony, since the differences between them are really superficial. The strategy is another example of pseudo-individuation. Song plugging on American radio, of course, is the well-known process by which new records are marketed by being aired over and over again. However, Adorno often speaks of "plugging the whole field." Top Forty listings and the Grammys are good examples of this. They are ways of giving the whole industry an undeserved sense of importance.

We have been speaking of the standardization of the music itself. Going hand in hand with this, Adorno believes, is the process by which the audience's *reactions* are standardized. Just as we are programmed to expect the standardized food at McDonald's, we are programmed to *expect* the music we get. (Adorno would reject the widely repeated claim that the commodity industry "only gives people what they want.") The two interrelated goals of this regimentation of human reactions, Adorno believes are: (a) to sell the product, and (b) to get audiences to identify with the system in which they live. The rewards for the consumer are cheap pleasures colored by escapist fantasies of freedom, and individuality. By means such as these, the commodity industry reconciles us to the capitalism in which we live, move, and have our being. (Adorno goes so far as to describe popular music as a means by which the system achieves "musical dictatorship" over the masses.) For the industry, there's another bonus: Our acceptance—indeed, our acquired need for—simplicity and repetition cuts down demands on the industry for genuine creativity. So, music producers need only make more of the very thing the industry has trained us to want. The consumers keep consuming and the music factories keep humming. It's a system, and it works.

A corollary to the foregoing is that popular music does not seriously *resist* the system. However, it must be made clear that Adorno does not regard explicit social protest in art as a very meaningful form of resistance. For one thing, such protest rarely gets to the basic issues that underlie surface symptoms. And Adorno would undoubtedly draw attention to the way the industry can take over superficial forms of resistance in order to give people the illusion of serious protest. (Consider the way fashion found it easy to co-opt and exploit the revolutionary images of, for example, Mao Tse Tung and Che Guevara.) For Adorno, serious artistic resistance is exemplified by the challenging abstract modernist music of composers like Arnold Schönberg or Alban

Berg. By its almost painful abstractness, such music holds out against the superficial pleasures of popular culture. True, idealizing views of jazz celebrate it as an expression of rebellion. Adorno claims, however, that the jazz musician actually lives in a hostile but basically "compliant" relationship to the system that promotes his music. He would undoubtedly say the same of rock music. Consider the way the cult of pop stardom overtakes "underground" bands such as Nirvana. Isn't commercial success always the underlying agenda?

In explaining how popular recordings work their way into the consciousness of listeners, Adorno has what he regards as a *psychological theory about the listener.* The effect of a record hit on a listener, he says, passes through a series of stages by which one is both figuratively and literally sold the music:

1. *Vague remembrance.* You hear a record on the radio and you say at first "I have heard something like this somewhere before."
2. *Actual identification.* At a second stage, you say, as Adorno puts it, "That's it!" You know *that* that tune is one you have heard before. A "light" of recognition goes on when you hear it the next time.
3. *Subsumption by label.* At this stage, you can assign a name to the tune or the band doing it. Or you may remember some of its lyrics. Taken together, stages one through three depend on and exploit the simple but seductive pleasure of sheer recognition.
4. *Self-reflection on the act of identification.* Helping himself to a psychoanalytic idea, Adorno believes that at a fourth stage you *identify* with the tune. You have a feeling that it is becoming part of you. Amidst the chaotic whirl of cultural commodities, you know your way with *this* item. However, Adorno also sees this stage as mobilizing certain social mechanisms. Adorno speaks here of a feeling of "safety in numbers." The record is bathed in the glow of group approval. You identify with the tune partly because it is acknowledged by others whom you esteem—your "in" group. This additionally sets you and your friends apart from the others who "haven't a clue." Adorno would have relished the modern disc jockey practice of playing records by request. When the DJ says: "This one goes out to Bob and Sally," it is as if the airwaves themselves acknowledge Bob and Sally's identification with that song. Bob and Sally, of course, say, "They're playing our song." The song is made for them—or so it seems.

   One might add that this stage undoubtedly brings, additionally, identifications with the pop stars themselves who perform the music. Although Adorno did not anticipate the extremes to which the modern cult of the pop star would be carried, he was certainly fascinated by our tendency to fixate on people whose *whole* value consists merely in their being acknowledged as stars. Recognition, one might say, becomes a sheer end in itself.
5. *Psychological transfer.* The internalization of the song becomes so tight that it amounts to a two-way relationship. Because the tune belongs so strongly to me, or to us, it acquires a glow of inherent value. It is judged to be good *in itself.* Clearly, Adorno regards this as a kind of illusion.

A further step in the psychological process does not appear in his numbered list in "On Popular Music," but his larger discussion justifies its inclusion:

6. *Disillusionment.* The shallowness of the music eventually becomes apparent. You are sick of it. The love affair is over. This stage has a social element too. You and your peer group feel a growing contempt for people who are behind you in this opinion. The tune is "corny," "out," "uncool," and so is anyone who still likes it. This final stage beautifully caps off the whole process. You are ready to buy a new CD. One could even add a further stage to Adorno's list. After a sufficient amount of time has passed, the record gets recycled as a "golden oldy," and the industry sells you the same old music a second time around. The re-packaging of the music of the Beatles in 1994–95—timed to coincide with the retrospective television coverage of the group's career—is a conspicuous example.

Consumers of pop music, on Adorno's account, are victims of enthusiasms that are "as ephemeral as seasonal styles." His view is challenging. However, it is overstated. For one thing, in making his contrast between popular and classical music, Adorno unfairly picks the worst examples of the former while focusing on the best examples of classical music. Tedious and banal examples of the latter abound. Further, disillusionment can set in with the "classics" no less than with popular music. Operas that were popular in the seventeenth century may please no one today at all. Played over and over again on "good music" stations—as it is!—even Beethoven's Fifth can become intolerable. Indeed, classical music, no less than pop, is subject to the pressures of the commodity industry. The popularity of trendy opera stars, no less than that of many pop stars, is the partial result of high-pressure advertising campaigns. The concert music industry, too, has ways of "plugging the field." Indeed, it is arguable that the "serious" music system creates a standardized kind of listener no less than the pop industry.

Adorno's view reflects two kinds of basic failings. First, he judges all music by the criteria of European classical music. Second, he sweeps all popular music down the drain—the best music of Cole Porter and George Gershwin along with the most cynical products of the industry. The two mistakes complement each other. It is because he lumps all popular music together that he is unable to make the kind of fine discriminations that are requisite for informed aesthetic judgments about popular music. Both problems are conspicuous in Adorno's treatment of jazz. They are undoubtedly responsible for his mistaken judgment that jazz cannot be resistant. Contrary to his implicit judgment, "submissive" is hardly a label we would apply to the art of Charlie Mingus, Ornette Coleman, or John Coltrane. The tragic tone of the latter's "Alabama" is surely as resistant as any music by Arnold Schönberg. To toss Coltrane's music into a heap with the most cynical products of the Time-Warner music industry would be laughable.

Adorno cannot help but object to jazz because he insists on measuring it by criteria applicable to classical music. For example, he claims that the reason we find the "bent" notes of jazz exciting is that our ear is moved to correct them back to the "right" notes. It is almost as if he hears jazz as if it *were* European music, but badly played, full of mistakes. Now the bent notes of which Adorno speaks here are probably those that reflect the tonality of the blues. The blues, be it noted, reflects the important interjection of non-European tonalities into European practice. In objecting to this feature of jazz, Adorno falls into a tonal chauvinism of the crudest sort. (What, after all, constitutes "right" notes in a world in which European tempered tonality is only one alternative among many?) Since Adorno cannot see the music in its own terms, he does not recognize that in jazz distinctive ways of handling musical materials, for example, rhythm, timbre, and spontaneity, are higher in the musical hierarchy than the musical characteristics of classical music. Because he is blind to these matters, he is incapable of making the kinds of discriminations that are necessary for understanding and appreciating jazz. His failure in this regard is certainly ironic, for he would be the first to fault musically illiterate listeners who do not make similarly refined discriminations within the sphere of classical music.

Adorno is right about the socio-economic pressures that bear on popular music. But he underestimates the degree to which it can transcend those conditions. However, to know this, he would have to be willing to judge various kinds of popular music on their own terms. There are, of course, important differences between the Rolling Stones and the Beatles, as anyone in the know can tell you.

Jokes

Ted Cohen

. . . If it is irrational to fail to be persuaded by a good argument, what is it to fail to be amused by a good joke? Not irrational, I think; certainly not in the same way. It is like being without taste. We will say 'irrational,' I think, not only of someone unpersuaded by a good argument, but also of someone who is unable to see that it *is* a good argument if the form is plainly valid and the premises obviously true. And we will, I think, deny a sense of humor not only in someone who isn't amused by the funniness he sees, but also in someone who can't see the funniness when it is clearly there.

What is a sense of humor? A capacity to be amused by the amusing, I suppose. What makes this capacity remarkable is that it is not coerced into activity. You don't *have* to laugh. Your response is not compelled in the way that an argument compels belief. Your response is not arbitrary, however. We don't all just happen coincidentally

An excerpt

to be laughing when we've heard a joke, as if we'd all simultaneously been tickled under the arms.

If I am correct, then the 'If—then' in 'If you hear a joke, then you laugh' stands for a relation we are poorly equipped to describe, for it is neither sternly logical nor merely contingent. Surely the joke must *cause* you to laugh, but it isn't the same as when tickling makes you laugh. It is exactly the relation Kant is ill-equipped to describe when he undertakes to analyze the judgment of taste. This judgment, he says, exhibits a response (to beauty) which is free but also somehow necessitated.

What is wrong with you if you are not amused, if you are not reached by this non-necessary, non-contingent relation? In escaping the proper response you are not so much wrong as different. It is not a trivial difference. It is a difference which leaves you outside a vital community, the community of those who feel this fun. It is a community which creates and acknowledges itself in the moment, and is powerless to conscript its membership. To fail to laugh at a joke is to remain outside that community. But you cannot will yourself in, any more than you can will yourself out.

A point in telling a joke is the attainment of community. There is special intimacy in shared laughter, and a mastering aim of joke-telling is the purveyance of this intimacy. The intimacy is most purified, refined, and uncluttered when the laughter is bound to the joke by the relation I have just been worrying over, a relation in which the laughter is not exacted but is nonetheless rendered fit. There are derivative forms of intimacy, in which the laughter is not so absolutely free. These obtain when the joke calls upon the background of the audience and uses this as a material condition for securing the effect. I think there are two main forms.

In the first form the joke is *hermetic.* It really makes sense only to those with special information, and the intimacy brought to those who qualify is bound up with a recognition—or re-recognition—that they do constitute an audience more select than humanity in general. The joke occasions the reconstitution of that select community. For an hermetic joke the required background may be very specific and decisive.

> What is Sacramento?
> It is the stuffing in a Catholic olive.

Either you know about pimento and the Church and its sacraments, and you get this joke, or you don't know these things and the joke is opaque. In America a very common device of this kind of joke is the incorporation of words or phrases in Yiddish. Appreciators of these jokes were once nearly restricted to certain Jews, but this has changed as an endless stream of Jewish comics forces more and more elements of Jewish humor, including vocabulary, on more and more of the general public.

Not every hermetic joke offers itself on this all-or-nothing basis. Some have depths which permit appreciation on different, if cumulative, levels.

> One day Toscanini was rehearsing the NBC Symphony. He stopped the playing to correct the trumpet line only to discover that the first-chair trumpet had intended exactly what he had played, and disagreed with Toscanini over how it should go. There ensued a heated argument which ended only when the trum-

peter stalked angrily off the stage. As he reached the wings he turned to Toscanini and said 'Schmuck!' The maestro replied, 'It's-a too late to apologize.'

If you know only the word 'Schmuck' you can manage this joke. In fact even if you don't know what it means you can sense enough from its phonetic quality to salvage the joke. But the more you know of professional musicians in New York, of Toscanini's ego and his peculiar approach to non-Roman language, and so on, the more you will make of the joke.

Here is a more intricate example of an hermetic joke.

A musician was performing a solo recital in Israel. When he ended the last selection, a thunderous response came from the audience, including many cries of 'Play it again.' He stepped forward, bowed, and said, 'What a wonderfully moving response. Of course I shall be delighted to play it again.' And he did. At the end, again there was a roar from the audience, and again many cries of 'Play it again.' This time the soloist came forward smiling and said, 'Thank you. I have never been so touched in all my concert career. I should love to play it again, but there is no time, for I must perform tonight in Tel Aviv. So, thank you from the bottom of my heart—and farewell.' Immediately a voice was heard from the back of the hall saying, 'You will stay here and play it again until you get it right.'

This joke works with nearly any audience, but its total riches are available only to those who know the Jewish religious requirement that on certain occasions the appropriate portion of the Hebrew Bible be read out, that those present make known any errors they detect in the reading, and that the reader not only acknowledge these corrections but that he then go back and read out the text correctly. That audience—those entirely within the community of this joke—will not only be able to find this extra level, but they should also find it a better joke. For them there is a point in the story's being set in Israel, and if there were no point in that, the joke would do better to omit the geography altogether.

In the second derivative form of intimacy the joke is likely to be rather simple, although not necessarily, and the background required is not one of knowledge but one of attitude or prejudice. I call these *affective* jokes. The most common examples are probably what in America are called ethnic jokes. It is not necessary that one actually believe that Jews are immoral, or Poles inept, or Italians lascivious, or whatever: indeed, most appreciators known to me have the opposite beliefs. What's needed is not a belief but a predisposition to enjoy situations in which Jews, Poles, Blacks, or whoever are singled out. . . .

The little schematism I've sketched divides jokes into two kinds, the pure ones and the conditional ones. The conditional ones, the ones the success of which requires a special background in the audience, are again divisible into two kinds: the hermetic ones, whose presumed background is one of knowledge or belief, and the affective ones, which require of the audience a particular prejudice, or feeling, or disposition, or inclination. (If you have a passion for this you might further divide the affective jokes into those for which the requisite predisposition is affirmative and those for which it is negative. In what Americans call a 'Polish' joke, the prejudice defames Poles. In Warsaw, however, a Polish joke is typically celebratory, and in the story a Pole subdues a Russian or a German or the Polish government.)

I am not saying that pure jokes are *better.* And they do not seem to be more interesting as a subject. Let me note two excellent topics associated with the complexity of conditional jokes.

First is the matter of active complicity. When your special background is called into play, your sensibility is galvanized. Something that sets you apart from just any person is brought into your apprehension and this adds to the quantity and alters the quality of the intimacy achieved. The point is like the one I think Aristotle has in mind when he declares the enthymeme the argument most suitable for certain kinds of persuasion. His idea is this: if you wish to set your audience in motion, especially with an eye toward provoking them to action, then you are well advised to induce them to supply the initial momentum themselves. You can do this by offering them an incomplete argument. They must then undertake a mental scramble in order to locate the premisses necessary to render the argument valid. This scramble is a motion of the mind undertaken *before* the legitimate arrival of the conclusion, and that motion augments the persuasion implicit in the validity of the completed argument. So it is, approximately, with conditional jokes. The requirement of a special background is not stated explicitly. The audience discovers that and it also discovers that it can supply what's needed. It is further aware that not everyone can supply the background (unlike an enthymeme's audience which potentially includes everyone because minimal logical acuity is enough to formulate the implicated missing premiss). In doing this the audience collaborates in the success of the joke—the constitution of intimacy—just as the audience for an enthymeme collaborates in the construction of a valid argument, with the difference that the audience of the joke derives additional intensity of feeling from knowing that the success is due to them specifically, that other groups would fail.

A second good topic concerning conditional jokes is the means they afford to a kind of fakery. A conditional joke demands a special contribution from the audience, either cognitive or affective. What if the joke-teller himself cannot supply this special constituent? In the first case, where the implicated background is cognitive, the teller is like a parrot, and he cannot himself know (find) what fun there is in the joke. This charlatan resembles a musician who doesn't divine the sense of a piece but nonetheless bangs it out note for note, or a religious practitioner who reads out texts or prayers in Latin or Hebrew, perhaps even 'with feeling,' but doesn't know what the words mean.

In the second case, where the requisite special contribution is a matter of feeling, the teller is more like a liar. He can, typically, find the fun—recognize it or identify it—but he cannot feel it. Perhaps the plainest examples of this insincerity are jokes told to groups of (say, racially) prejudiced people—genuine bigots, that is—by one who does not share the true depths of the bigotry but means to ingratiate himself with the group. This is a kind of fraudulence, like that of the man who says 'I apologize' without feeling sorry, of the artist who mimics unfelt forms, and of the performer who does not feel the passion in the scores he plays with mindless virtuosity.

The two kinds of fakery are different. The first is, mainly, simply bizarre. The second is more devious, even deceitful. In both, however, there is the fraudulence of emptiness, as both betray the commitment to intimacy I have characterized as a kind of generic aim of joke-telling. The teller of these jokes is inauthentic: he invites and even induces you into a putative community in which he himself has no place. Who is he to be issuing these invitations?

The difference between pure and conditional jokes corresponds to a difference in moral and religious conceptions. The idea of a pure joke rests on a conviction that at some level people are essentially the same and can all be reached by the same device. This is, perhaps, a fundamentally Christian idea. The denial of the possibility of a pure joke rests on a conviction that people are essentially different, or at least that they belong to essentially different groups. The idea that all jokes necessarily are conditional seems to me a kind of Jewish idea (not the only kind).

Those who believe only in conditional jokes will concede that it is possible to appreciate a joke whose community does not include oneself. How is this possible? It must be through an act of imagination which transports one into the relevant community. Thus I can appreciate jokes meant for women, Englishmen, and mathematicians, although I am none of those. There is a point, however, at which it becomes impossible for me to be amused. I reach that point sooner when the joke is anti-Jewish or anti-American than when it is anti-women or anti-English. And there is a point for any type of affective joke beyond which its instances are objectionable. They are in bad taste. If you think that lapses of 'taste' are always relatively innocuous, then I would insist that these jokes are in fact unacceptable—immoral. Why does this happen, and when?

I cannot give a complete answer, even in outline, because there is a fundamental question I do not know how to answer. Suppose that *x* is some real event, and that it is (morally) unacceptable to laugh at *x*. The question I cannot answer is, under what conditions is it wrong to laugh at a fictional report of *x*, and why? It may be that a heavy traffic of amusement in *x*-jokes creates or reinforces beliefs or attitudes that are themselves objectionable or that lead to intolerable acts. That answer is insufficient, for two reasons. First, there is little evidence to show that it is always true, and some indication that it is sometimes false. Second, it doesn't get to the heart of the evil, even if it is true, for even if it could be demonstrated that these jokes lead to no bad ends the jokes themselves would still be offensive. With no good answer to the question of why (and when) it is wrong to laugh at a story of something you shouldn't laugh at, I shall nevertheless go on to suggest how an answer—if we had one—might lead to an understanding of the unacceptability of some jokes.

Suppose that prejudice against *P*'s is a bad thing, and that to be amused by an *x*-joke requires a disposition which is related to anti-*P* prejudice, although that disposition is not itself a prejudice. The joke will be accessible only to those who either have the disposition or can, in imagination, respond as if they had it. The joke is obviously conditional—it is affective; but it will also be fundamentally parochial (essentially conditional, one might say) if there are people who cannot find it accessible. What people will be in this position? *P*'s, I think. Even the imagined possession of the disposition is in conflict with what makes these people *P*'s. To appreciate the joke a *P* must disfigure himself. He must forsake himself. He should not do that. In fact he cannot do that while remaining a *P*. The rest of us, who are not *P*'s, *should* not appreciate the joke although we *can* in this sense in which a *P* cannot. The joke is viciously exclusionary, and it should be resisted.

What this implies depends upon exactly what people essentially are. Are they essentially men or women, of some race, of some age, of some religion, of some profession, of some size? That is a fine question in the metaphysics of morality, and one I do not care to answer here. I offer this account of a kind of unacceptable joke as an explanation and justification of why some people find some jokes intolerable. A currently common exchange begins with a man telling a joke (involving women, typically) which a woman finds offensive. She objects and is told she has no sense of humor. Her reply could be that she cannot bring her sense of humor to that joke without imaginatively taking on a disposition which is incompatible with her conception of herself as a woman or a certain kind of woman. And if she is essentially a woman or a certain kind of woman, then she cannot reach the joke without a hideous cost.

Although the basis for a pure joke has an obvious moral flavor, akin to the idea of a universal human sameness, conditional jokes are also congenial to the serious idea of morality. Conditional jokes are related to the idea that we can respect and even appreciate one another while remaining irreducibly different. They carry a danger, however, for their parochialism easily becomes unbearably sectarian.

A final note about pure jokes. The major question, I suppose, is whether there are any. If there are, they will be jokes whose presumptive success depends on nothing whatever. The audience need no special background. They bring to the joke only their humanity. Now the question is, When you tell such a joke, upon what basis do you expect anyone else to be moved? The answer must be, Upon the fact that the joke moves you, plus your estimate that it moves you simply as a person and without regard to any idiosyncracy of yours. The logic here is exactly the same as that which Kant cites in answering the question, By what right do you judge anything to be beautiful (where this means, Upon what basis do you suppose that anyone else should take pleasure in this thing?)? Kant answers: Upon the fact that the object pleases you, plus your estimate that the pleasure is due to nothing about you beyond the fact that you are a person.

But now comes the nasty question, which Kant believes he can answer with regard to the beauty of things, and I am not so sure about with regard to the funniness of jokes. If a thing touches you, so to speak, only in the rudiments of your person—if ever such a thing happens, with all those things dormant which make you more than just a person; why should it be good as well for any other rudimentary person? Isn't there room within even the most elementary, stripped-down, homogenized human sensibility for variation? Couldn't you and I be mere men and nothing more, and yet be pleased by different beauties and laugh at different jokes? No, says Kant, in the first instance, for the capacity to feel this pleasure is identical with the capacity which makes knowledge possible (and knowledge *is* possible, he insists interminably). And so there is an argument, however good.

Is there such an argument for the postulation of a universal sense of humor? I do not know. Is the capacity to find a joke funny a basic, essential feature of our sensibility? It needn't seem entirely implausible that it is if we suppose it to be, minimally—and it is only its minimal presence that matters—the capacity to feel simultaneously the appropriateness and the absurdity of a punch line. It is like feeling the wonderful hopelessness of the world. (Or is it the hopeless wonder of the world?) But must every one of us have within himself the capacity for that feeling, however disfigured it may have become? God knows.

The sudden click at the end of a certain kind of joke is its hallmark. There is an unexpected, an almost-but-not-quite-predicted coincidence of moments. And this is part of a marvelous reflexivity. Earlier I guessed that the whole joke relates to its effect in an enigmatic relation which renders that effect both unforced and fitting. The relation can be found again entirely within the joke. The joke itself has a beginning which leads to an end which is unforced (and so, unpredicted), but altogether right. In laughing we fit ourselves to a joke just as its punch line fits to its body, by this relation of self-warranting propriety. It is a kind of mirroring. We find ourselves reflected in a surface which mirrors our dearest and perhaps most human hope: to do well, but not under compulsion. A joke shows us that and shows us doing that. Anything which can show us that aspect of ourselves deserves fond and serious attention.

Pornography

Joel Feinberg

. . . Rape is a harm and a severe one. Harm prevention is definitely a legitimate use of the criminal law. Therefore, if there is a clear enough causal connection to rape, a statute that prohibits violent pornography would be a morally legitimate restriction of liberty. But it is not enough to warrant suppression that pornography as a whole might have some harmful consequences to third parties, even though most specific instances of it do not. "Communications from other human beings are among the most important causes of human behavior," Kent Greenawalt points out, "but criminal law cannot concern itself with every communication that may fortuitously lead to the commission of a crime. It would, for example, be ludicrous to punish a supervisor for criticizing a subordinate, even if it could be shown that the criticism so inflamed the subordinate that he assaulted a fellow worker hours later." An even stronger point can be made. Even where there is statistical evidence that a certain percentage of

---

An excerpt

communications of a given type will predictably lead the second party to harm third parties, so that in a sense the resultant harms are not "fortuitous," that is not sufficient warrant for prohibiting all communications of that kind. It would be even more ludicrous, for example for a legislature to pass a criminal statute against the criticism of subordinates, on the ground that inflamed employees sometimes become aggressive with their fellow workers.

A more relevant example of the same point, and one with an ironic twist, is provided by Fred Berger:

> A journal that has published studies often cited by the radical feminists . . . has also published an article that purports to show that the greater emancipation of women in western societies has led to great increases in criminal activity *by* women. Such crimes as robbery, larceny, burglary, fraud, and extortion have shown marked increase, as have arson, murder, and aggravated assault. But freedom of expression would mean little if such facts could be taken as a reason to suppress expression that seeks the further liberation of women from their secondary, dependent status with respect to men.

Of course, one can deny that violent porn is a form of valuable free expression analogous to scholarly feminist articles, but the point remains that indirectly produced harms are not by themselves sufficient grounds for criminalizing materials, that some further conditions must be satisfied.

Those instances of sexual violence which may be harmful side-effects of violent pornography are directly produced by criminals (rapists) acting voluntarily on their own. We already have on the statute books a firm prohibition of rape and sexual assault. If, in addition, the harm principle permits the criminalization of actions only indirectly related to the primary harm, such as producing, displaying or selling violent pornography, then there is a danger that the law will be infected with unfairness; for unless certain further conditions are fulfilled, the law will be committed to punishing some parties for the entirely voluntary criminal conduct of other parties. . . . Suppose that *A* wrongfully harms (e.g. rapes) *B* in circumstances such that (1) *A* acts fully voluntarily on his own initiative, and (2) nonetheless, but for what *C* has communicated to him, he would not have done what he did to *B*. Under what further conditions, we must ask, can *C* be rightfully held criminally responsible along with *A* for the harm to *B?* Clearly *C* can be held responsible if the information he communicated was helpful assistance to *A* and intended to be such. In that case *C* becomes a kind of collaborator. Under traditional law, *C* can also incur liability if what he communicated to *A* was some kind of encouragement to commit a crime against *B*. The clearest cases are those in which *C* solicits *A*'s commission of the criminal act by offering inducements to him. "Encouragement" is also criminal when it takes the form of active urging. Sometimes mere advice to commit the act counts as an appropriate sort of encouragement. When the encouragement takes a general form, and the harmful crime is recommended to "the general reader" or an indefinite audience, then the term "advocacy" is often used. Advocating criminal conduct is arguably a way of producing such conduct, and is thus often itself a crime. An article in a pornographic magazine advocating the practice of rape (as opposed to advocating a legislative change of the rape laws) would presumably be a crime if its intent were serious and its audience presumed to be impressionable to an appropriately dangerous degree.

Violent pornography, however, does not seem to fit any of these models. Its authors and vendors do not solicit rapes; nor do they urge or advise rapes; nor do they advocate rape. If some of their customers, some of the time, might yet "find encouragement" in their works to commit rapes because rape has been portrayed in a way that happens to be alluring to them, that is their own affair, the pornographer might insist, and their own responsibility. The form of "encouragement" that is most applicable (if any are) to the pornography case is that which the common law has traditionally called "incitement." Sir Edward Coke wrote in 1628 that "all those that incite . . . set on, or stir up any other" to a crime are themselves accessories. Thus, haranguing an angry crowd on the doorsteps of a corn dealer, in Mill's famous example, might be the spark that incites the mob's violence against the hated merchant, even though the speaker did not explicitly urge, advise, or advocate it. Yet, a similar speech, twenty-four hours earlier, to a calmer audience in a different location, though it may have made a causal contribution to the eventual violence, would not have borne a close enough relation to the harm to count as an "incitement," or "positive instigation" (Mill's term) of it.

Given that "communication" is a form of expression, and thus has an important social value, obviously it cannot rightly be made criminal simply on the ground that it may lead some others on their own to act harmfully. Even if works of pure pornography are *not* to be treated as "communication," "expression," or "speech" (in the sense of the first amendment), but as mere symbolic aphrodisiacs or sex aids without further content they may yet have an intimate personal value to those who use them, and a social value derived from the importance we attach to the protection of private erotic experience. By virtue of that significance, one person's liberty can be invaded to prevent the harm other parties might cause to *their* victims only when the invaded behavior has a specially direct connection to the harm caused, something perhaps like direct "incitement." Fred Berger suggests three necessary conditions that expected harms must satisfy if they are to justify censorship or prohibition of erotic materials, none of which, he claims, is satisfied by pornography, even violent pornography.

1. There must be strong evidence of a very likely and serious harm. [I would add—"that would not have occurred otherwise."]
2. The harms must be clearly and directly linked with the expression.
3. It must be unlikely that further speech or expression can be used effectively to combat the harm.

Berger suggests that the false shout of "fire" in a crowded theatre is paradigmatically the kind of communication that satisfies these conditions. If so, then he must interpret the second condition to be something like the legal standard of incitement—setting on, stirring up, inflaming the other party (or mob of parties) to the point of hysteria or panic, so that their own infliction of the subsequent damage is something less than deliberate and fully voluntary. Their inciter in that case is as responsible as they are, perhaps even more so, for the harm that ensues. Surely, the relation between pornographers and rapists is nowhere near that direct and manipulative. If it were, we would punish the pornographers proportionately more severely, and blame the actual rapist (poor chap; he was "inflamed") proportionately less.

It may yet happen that further evidence will show that Berger's conditions, or some criteria similar to them, are satisfied by violent pornography. In that case, a liberal should have no hesitation in using the criminal law to prevent the harm. In the meantime, the appropriate liberal response should be a kind of uneasy skepticism about the harmful effects of pornography on third party victims, conjoined with increasingly energetic use of "further speech or expression" against the cult of macho, "effectively to combat the harm." . . .

Art as Experience

John Dewey

Experience occurs continuously, because the interaction of live creature and environing conditions is involved in the very process of living. Under conditions of resistance and conflict, aspects and elements of the self and the world that are implicated in this interaction qualify experience with emotions and ideas so that conscious intent emerges. Oftentimes, however, the experience had is inchoate. Things are experienced but not in such a way that they are composed into *an* experience. There is distraction and dispersion; what we observe and what we think, what we desire and what we get, are at odds with each other. We put our hands to the plow and turn back; we start and then we stop, not because the experience has reached the end for the sake of which it was initiated but because of extraneous interruptions or of inner lethargy.

In contrast with such experience, we have *an* experience when the material experienced runs its course to fulfillment. Then and then only is it integrated within and demarcated in the general stream of experience from other experiences. A piece of work is finished in a way that is satisfactory; a problem receives its solution; a game is played through; a situation, whether that of eating a meal, playing a game of chess, carrying on a conversation, writing a book, or taking part in a political campaign, is so rounded out that its close is a consummation and not a cessation. Such an experience is a whole and carries with it its own idividualizing quality and self-sufficiency. It is *an* experience.

An excerpt

Philosophers, even empirical philosophers, have spoken for the most part of experience at large. Idiomatic speech, however, refers to experiences each of which is singular, having its own beginning and end. For life is no uniform uninterrupted march or flow. It is a thing of histories, each with its own plot, its own inception and movement toward its close, each having its own particular rhythmic movement; each with its own unrepeated quality pervading it throughout. A flight of stairs, mechanical as it is, proceeds by individualized steps, not by undifferentiated progression, and an inclined plane is at least marked off from other things by abrupt discreteness.

Experience in this vital sense is defined by those situations and episodes that we spontaneously refer to as being "real experiences"; those things of which we say in recalling them, "that *was* an experience." It may have been something of tremendous importance—a quarrel with one who was once an intimate, a catastrophe finally averted by a hair's breadth. Or it may have been something that in comparison was slight—and which perhaps because of its very slightness illustrates all the better what is to be an experience. There is that meal in a Paris restaurant of which one says "that *was* an experience." It stands out as an enduring memorial of what food may be. Then there is that storm one went through in crossing the Atlantic—the storm that seemed in its fury, as it was experienced, to sum up in itself all that a storm can be, complete in itself, standing out because marked out from what went before and what came after.

In such experiences, every successive part flows freely, without seam and without unfilled blanks, into what ensues. At the same time there is no sacrifice of the self-identity of the parts. A river, as distinct from a pond, flows. But its flow gives a definiteness and interest to its successive portions greater than exist in the homogenous portions of a pond. In an experience, flow is from something to something. As one part leads into another and as one part carries on what went before, each gains distinctness in itself. The enduring whole is diversified by successive phases that are emphases of its varied colors.

Because of continuous merging, there are no holes, mechanical junctions, and dead centers when we have *an* experience. There are pauses, places of rest, but they punctuate and define the quality of movement. They sum up what has been undergone and prevent its dissipation and idle evaporation. Continued acceleration is breathless and prevents parts from gaining distinction. In a work of art, different acts, episodes, occurrences melt and fuse into unity, and yet do not disappear and lose their own character as they do so—just as in a genial conversation there is a continuous interchange and blending, and yet each speaker not only retains his own character but manifests it more clearly than is his wont.

An experience has a unity that gives it its name, *that* meal, that storm, that rupture of friendship. The existence of this unity is constituted by a single *quality* that pervades the entire experience in spite of the variation of its constituent parts. This unity is neither emotional, practical, nor intellectual, for these terms name distinctions that reflection can make within it. In discourse *about* an experience, we must make use of these adjectives of interpretation. In going over an experience in mind *after* its occurrence, we may find that one property rather than another was sufficiently dominant so that it characterizes the experience as a whole. There are absorbing inquiries and speculations which a scientific man and philosopher will recall as "experiences" in the emphatic sense. In final import they are intellectual. But in their actual occurrence they were emotional as well; they were purposive and volitional. Yet the experience was not a sum of these different characters; they were lost in it as distinctive traits. No thinker can ply his occupation save as he is lured and rewarded by total integral experiences that are intrinsically worth while. Without them he would never know what it is really to think and would be completely at a loss in distinguishing real thought from the spurious article. Thinking goes on in trains of ideas, but the ideas form a train only because they are much more than what an analytic psychology calls ideas. They are phases, emotionally and practically distinguished, of a developing underlying quality; they are its moving variations, not separate and independent like Locke's and Hume's so-called ideas and impressions, but are subtle shadings of a pervading and developing hue.

We say of an experience of thinking that we reach or draw a conclusion. Theoretical formulation of the process is often made in such terms as to conceal effectually the similarity of "conclusion" to the consummating phase of every developing integral experience. These formulations apparently take their cue from the separate propositions that are premises and the proposition that is the conclusion as they appear on the printed page. The impression is derived that there are first two independent and ready-made entities that are then manipulated so as to give rise to a third. In fact, in an experience of thinking, premises emerge only as a conclusion becomes manifest. The experience, like that of watching a storm reach its height and gradually subside, is one of continuous movement of subject-matters. Like the ocean in the storm, there are a series of waves; suggestions reaching out and being broken in a clash, or being carried onwards by a coöperative wave. If a conclusion is reached, it is that of a movement of anticipation and cumulation, one that finally comes to completion. A "conclusion" is no separate and independent thing; it is the consummation of a movement.

Hence *an* experience of thinking has its own esthetic quality. It differs from those experiences that are acknowledged to be esthetic, but only in its materials. The material of the fine arts consists of qualities; that of experience having intellectual conclusion are signs or symbols having no intrinsic quality of their own, but standing for things that may in another experience be qualitatively experienced. The difference is enormous. It is one reason why the strictly intellectual art will never be popular as music is popular. Nevertheless, the experience itself has a satisfying emotional quality because it possesses internal integration and fulfillment reached through ordered and organized movement. This artistic structure may be immediately felt. In so far, it is esthetic. What is even more important is that not only is this quality a significant motive in undertaking intellectual inquiry and in keeping it honest, but that no intellectual activity is an integral event (is *an* experience), unless it is rounded out with this quality. Without it, thinking is inconclusive. In short, esthetic cannot be sharply marked off from intellectual experience since the latter must bear an esthetic stamp to be itself complete. . . .

Thus the non-esthetic lies within two limits. At one pole is the loose succession that does not begin at any particular place and that ends—in the sense of ceasing—at no particular place. At the other pole is arrest, constriction, proceeding from parts having only a mechanical connection with one another. There exists so much of one and the other of these two kinds of experience that unconsciously they come to be taken as norms of all experience. Then, when the esthetic appears, it so sharply contrasts with the picture that has been formed of experience, that it is impossible to combine its special qualities with the features of the picture and the esthetic is given an outside place and status. The account that has been given of experience dominantly intellectual and practical is intended to show that there is no such contrast involved in having an experience; that, on the contrary, no experience of whatever sort is a unity unless it has esthetic quality.

The enemies of the esthetic are neither the practical nor the intellectual. They are the humdrum; slackness of loose ends; submission to convention in practice and intellectual procedure. Rigid abstinence, coerced submission, tightness on one side and dissipation, incoherence and aimless indulgence on the other, are deviations in opposite directions from the unity of an experience. Some such considerations perhaps induced Aristotle to invoke the "mean proportional" as the proper designation of what is distinctive of both virtue and the esthetic. He was formally correct. "Mean" and "proportion" are, however, not self-explanatory, nor to be taken over in a prior mathematical sense, but are properties belonging to an experience that has a developing movement toward its own consummation.

I have emphasized the fact that every integral experience moves toward a close, an ending, since it ceases only when the energies active in it have done their proper work. This closure of a circuit of energy is the opposite of arrest, of *stasis.* Maturation and fixation are polar opposites. Struggle and conflict may be themselves enjoyed, although they are painful, when they are experienced as means of developing an experience; members in that they carry it forward, not just because they are there. There is, as will appear later, an element of undergoing, of suffering in its large sense, in every experience. Otherwise there would be no taking in of what preceded. For "taking in" in any vital experience is something more than placing something on the top of consciousness over what was previously known. It involves reconstruction which may be painful. Whether the necessary undergoing phase is by itself pleasurable or painful is a matter of particular conditions. It is indifferent to the total esthetic quality, save that there are few intense esthetic experiences that are wholly gleeful. They are certainly not to be characterized as amusing, and as they bear down upon us they involve a suffering that is none the less consistent with, indeed a part of, the complete perception that is enjoyed.

I have spoken of the esthetic quality that rounds out an experience into completeness and unity as emotional. The reference may cause difficulty. We are given to thinking of emotions as things as simple and compact as are the words by which we name them. Joy, sorrow, hope, fear, anger, curiosity, are treated as if each in itself were a sort of entity that enters full-made upon the scene, an entity that may last a long time or a short time, but whose duration, whose growth and career, is irrelevant to its nature. In fact emotions are qualities, when they are significant, of a complex experience that moves and changes. I say, when they are *significant,* for otherwise they are but the outbreaks and eruptions of a disturbed infant. All emotions are qualifications of a drama and they change as the drama develops. Persons are sometimes said to fall in love at first sight. But what they fall into is not a thing of that instant. What would love be were it compressed into a moment in which there is no room for cherishing and for solicitude? The intimate nature of emotion is manifested in the experience of one watching a play on the stage or reading a novel. It attends the development of a plot; and a plot requires a stage, a space, wherein to develop and time in which to unfold. Experience is emotional but there are no separate things called emotions in it.

By the same token, emotions are attached to events and objects in their movement. They are not, save in pathological instances, private. And even an "objectless" emotion demands something beyond itself to which to attach itself, and thus it soon generates a delusion in lack of something real. Emotion belongs of a certainty to the self. But it belongs to the self that is concerned in the movement of events toward an issue that is desired or disliked. We jump instantaneously when we are scared, as we blush on the instant when we are ashamed. But fright and shamed modesty are not in this case emotional states. Of themselves they are but automatic reflexes. In order to become emotional they must become parts of an inclusive and enduring situation that involves concern for objects and their issues. The jump of fright becomes emotional fear when there is found or thought to exist a threatening object that must be dealt with or escaped from. The blush becomes the emotion of shame when a person connects, in thought, an action he has performed with an unfavorable reaction to himself of some other person.

Physical things from far ends of the earth are physically transported and physically caused to act and react upon one another in the construction of a new object. The miracle of mind is that something similar takes place in experience without physical transport and assembling. Emotion is the moving and cementing force. It selects what is congruous and dyes what is selected with its color, thereby giving qualitative unity to materials externally disparate and dissimilar. It thus provides unity in and through the varied parts of an experience. When the unity is of the sort already described, the experience has esthetic character even though it is not, dominantly, an esthetic experience. . . .

The Role of Theory in Aesthetics

Morris Weitz

. . . Is aesthetic theory, in the sense of a true definition or set of necessary and sufficient properties of art, possible? If nothing else does, the history of aesthetics itself should give one enormous pause here. For, in spite of the many theories, we seem no nearer our goal today than we were in Plato's time. Each age, each art-movement, each philosophy of art, tries over and over again to establish the stated ideal only to be succeeded by a new or revised theory, rooted, at least in part, in the repudiation of preceding ones. Even today, almost everyone interested in aesthetic matters is still deeply wedded to the hope that the correct theory of art is forthcoming. We need only examine the numerous new books on art in which new definitions are proffered; or, in our own country especially, the basic textbooks and anthologies to recognize how strong the priority of a theory of art is.

In this essay I want to plead for the rejection of this problem. I want to show that theory—in the requisite classical sense—is *never* forthcoming in aesthetics, and that we would do much better as philosophers to supplant the question, "What is the nature of art?," by other questions, the answers to which will provide us with all the understanding of the arts there can be. I want to show that the inadequacies of the theories are not primarily occasioned by any legitimate difficulty such e.g., as the vast complexity of art, which might be corrected by further probing and research. Their basic inadequacies reside instead in a fundamental misconception of art. Aesthetic theory—all of it—is wrong in principle in thinking that a correct theory is possible because it radically misconstrues the logic of the concept of art. Its main contention that "art" is amenable to real or any kind of true definition is false. Its attempt to discover the necessary and sufficient properties of art is logically misbegotten for the very simple reason that such a set and, consequently, such a formula about it, is never forthcoming. Art, as the logic of the concept shows, has no set of necessary and sufficient properties, hence a theory of it is logically impossible and not merely factually difficult. Aesthetic theory tries to define what cannot be defined in its requisite sense. But in recommending the repudiation of aesthetic theory I shall not argue from this, as too many others have done, that its logical confusions render it meaningless or worthless. On the contrary, I wish to reassess its role and its contribution primarily in order to show that it is of the greatest importance to our understanding of the arts.

Let us now survey briefly some of the more famous extant aesthetic theories in order to see if they do incorporate correct and adequate statements about the nature

---

An excerpt

of art. In each of these there is the assumption that it is the true enumeration of the defining properties of art, with the implication that previous theories have stressed wrong definitions. Thus, to begin with, consider a famous version of Formalist theory, that propounded by Bell and Fry. It is true that they speak mostly of painting in their writings but both assert that what they find in that art can be generalized for what is "art" in the others as well. The essence of painting, they maintain, are the plastic elements in relation. Its defining property is significant form, i.e., certain combinations of lines, colors, shapes, volumes—everything on the canvas except the representational elements—which evoke a unique response to such combinations. Painting is definable as plastic organization. The nature of art, what it *really* is, so their theory goes, is a unique combination of certain elements (the specifiable plastic ones) in their relations. Anything which is art is an instance of significant form; and anything which is not art has no such form.

To this the Emotionalist replies that the truly essential property of art has been left out. Tolstoy, Ducasse, or any of the advocates of this theory, find that the requisite defining property is not significant form but rather the expression of emotion in some sensuous public medium. Without projection of emotion into some piece of stone or words or sounds, etc., there can be no art. Art is really such embodiment. It is this that uniquely characterizes art, and any true, real definition of it, contained in some adequate theory of art, must so state it.

The Intuitionist disclaims both emotion and form as defining properties. In Croce's version, for example, art is identified not with some physical, public object but with a specific creative, cognitive and spiritual act. Art is really a first stage of knowledge in which certain human beings (artists) bring their images and intuitions into lyrical clarification or expression. As such, it is an awareness, non-conceptual in character, of the unique individuality of things; and since it exists below the level of conceptualization or action, it is without scientific or moral content. Croce singles out as the defining essence of art this first stage of spiritual life and advances its identification with art as a philosophically true theory or definition.

The Organicist says to all of this that art is really a class of organic wholes consisting of distinguishable, albeit inseparable, elements in their causally efficacious relations which are presented in some sensuous medium. In A. C. Bradley, in piece-meal versions of it in literary criticism, or in my own generalized adaptation of it in my *Philosophy of the Arts,* what is claimed is that anything which is a work of art is in its nature a unique complex of interrelated parts—in painting, for example, lines, colors, volumes, subjects, etc., all interacting upon one another on a paint surface of some sort. Certainly, at one time at least it seemed to me that this organic theory constituted the one true and real definition of art.

My final example is the most interesting of all, logically speaking. This is the Voluntarist theory of [DeWitt] Parker. In his writings on art, Parker persistently calls into question the traditional simple-minded definitions of aesthetics. "The assumption underlying every philosophy of art is the existence of some common nature present in all the arts." "All the so popular brief definitions of art—'significant form,' 'expression,' 'intuition,' 'objectified pleasure'—are fallacious, either because, while true of art, they are also true of much that is not art, and hence fail to differentiate art from other things; or else because they neglect some essential aspect of art." But instead of inveighing against the attempt at definition of art itself, Parker insists that what is needed is a complex definition rather than a simple one. "The definition of art must therefore be in terms of a complex of characteristics. Failure to recognize this has been the fault of all the well-known definitions." His own version of Voluntarism is the theory that art is essentially three things: embodiment of wishes and desires imaginatively satisfied, language, which characterizes the public medium of art, and harmony, which unifies the language with the layers of imaginative projections. Thus, for Parker, it is a true definition to say of art that it is ". . . the provision of satisfaction through the imagination, social significance, and harmony. I am claiming that nothing except works of art possesses all three of these marks."

Now, all of these sample theories are inadequate in many different ways. Each purports to be a complete statement about the defining features of all works of art and yet each of them leaves out something which the others take to be central. Some are circular, e.g., the Bell-Fry theory of art as significant form which is defined in part in terms of our response to significant form. Some of them, in their search for necessary and sufficient properties, emphasize too few properties, like (again) the Bell-Fry definition which leaves out subject-representation in painting, or the Croce theory which omits inclusion of the very important feature of the public, physical character, say, of architecture. Others are too general and cover objects that are not art as well as works of art. Organicism is surely such a view since it can be applied to *any* causal unity in the natural world as well as to art. Still others rest on dubious principles, e.g., Parker's claim that art embodies imaginative satisfactions, rather than real ones; or Croce's assertion that there is nonconceptual knowledge. Consequently, even if art has one set of necessary and sufficient properties, none of the theories we have noted or, for that matter, no aesthetic theory yet proposed, has enumerated that set to the satisfaction of all concerned.

Then there is a different sort of difficulty. As real definitions, these theories are supposed to be factual reports on art. If they are, may we not ask, Are they empirical and open to verification or falsification? For example, what would confirm or disconfirm the theory that art is significant form or embodiment of emotion or creative synthesis of images? There does not even seem to be a hint of the kind of evidence which might be forthcoming to test these theories; and indeed one wonders if they are perhaps honorific definitions of "art," that is, proposed redefinitions in terms of some *chosen* conditions for applying the concept of art, and not true or false reports on the essential properties of art at all.

But all these criticisms of traditional aesthetic theories—that they are circular, incomplete, untestable, pseudo-factual, disguised proposals to change the meaning of concepts—have been made before. My intention is to go beyond these to make a much more fundamental criticism, namely, that aesthetic theory is a logically vain attempt to define what cannot be defined, to state the necessary and sufficient properties of that which has no necessary and sufficient properties, to conceive the concept of art as closed when its very use reveals and demands its openness.

The problem with which we must begin is not "What is art?," but "What sort of concept is 'art'?" Indeed, the root problem of philosophy itself is to explain the relation between the employment of certain kinds of concepts and the conditions under which they can be correctly applied. If I may paraphrase Wittgenstein, we must not ask, What is the nature of any philosophical x?, or even, according to the semanticist, What does "x" mean?, a transformation that leads to the disastrous interpretation of "art" as a name for some specifiable class of objects; but rather, What is the use or employment of "x"? What does "x" do in the language? This, I take it, is the initial question, the begin-all if not the end-all of any philosophical problem and solution. Thus, in aesthetics, our first problem is the elucidation of the actual employment of the concept of art, to give a logical description of the actual functioning of the concept, including a description of the conditions under which we correctly use it or its correlates.

My model in this type of logical description or philosophy derives from Wittgenstein. It is also he who, in his refutation of philosophical theorizing in the sense of constructing definitions of philosophical entities, has furnished contemporary aesthetics with a starting point for any future progress. In his new work, *Philosophical Investigations,* Wittgenstein raises as an illustrative question, What is a game? The traditional philosophical, theoretical answer would be in terms of some exhaustive set of properties common to all games. To this Wittgenstein says, let us consider what we call "games": "I mean board-games, card-games, ball-games, Olympic games, and so on. What is common to them all?—Don't say: 'there *must* be something common, or they would not be called "games"' but *look and see* whether there is anything common to all.—For if you look at them you will not see something that is common to *all,* but similarities, relationships, and a whole series of them at that . . ."

Card games are like board games in some respects but not in others. Not all games are amusing, nor is there always winning or losing or competition. Some games resemble others in some respects—that is all. What we find are no necessary and sufficient properties, only "a complicated network of similarities overlapping and criss-crossing," such that we can say of games that they form a family with family resemblances and no common trait. If one asks what a game is, we pick out sample games, describe these, and add, "This and *similar things* are called 'games'." This is all we need to say and indeed all any of us knows about games. Knowing what a game is is not knowing some real definition or theory but being able to recognize and explain games and to decide which among imaginary and new examples would or would not be called "games."

The problem of the nature of art is like that of the nature of games, at least in these respects: If we actually look and see what it is that we call "art," we will also find no common properties—only strands of similarities. Knowing what art is is not apprehending some manifest or latent essence but being able to recognize, describe, and explain those things we call "art" in virtue of these similarities.

But the basic resemblance between these concepts is their open texture. In elucidating them, certain (paradigm) cases can be given, about which there can be no question as to their being correctly described as "art" or "game," but no exhaustive set of cases can be given. I can list some cases and some conditions under which I can apply correctly the concept of art but I cannot list all of them, for the all-important reason that unforeseeable or novel conditions are always forthcoming or envisageable.

A concept is open if its conditions of application are emendable and corrigible; i.e., if a situation or case can be imagined or secured which would call for some sort of *decision* on our part to extend the use of the concept to cover this, or to close the concept and invent a new one to deal with the new case and its new property. If necessary and sufficient conditions for the application of a concept can be stated, the concept is a closed one. But this can happen only in logic or mathematics where concepts are constructed and completely defined. It cannot occur with empirically-descriptive and normative concepts unless we arbitrarily close them by stipulating the ranges of their uses. . . .

"Art," itself, is an open concept. New conditions (cases) have constantly arisen and will undoubtedly constantly arise; new art forms, new movements will emerge, which will demand decisions on the part of those interested, usually professional critics, as to whether the concept should be extended or not. Aestheticians may lay down similarity conditions but never necessary and sufficient ones for the correct application of the concept. With "art" its conditions of application can never be exhaustively enumerated since new cases can always be envisaged or created by artists, or even nature, which would call for a decision on someone's part to extend or to close the old or to invent a new concept. (E.g., "It's not a sculpture, it's a mobile.")

What I am arguing, then, is that the very expansive, adventurous character of art, its ever-present changes and novel creations, makes it logically impossible to ensure any set of defining properties. We can, of course, choose to close the concept. But to do this with "art" or "tragedy" or "portraiture," etc., is ludicrous since it forecloses on the very conditions of creativity in the arts. . . .

As we actually use the concept, "Art" is both descriptive (like "chair") and evaluative (like "good"); i.e., we sometimes say, "This is a work of art," to describe something and we sometimes say it to evaluate something. Neither use surprises anyone. . . .

The elucidation of the descriptive use of "Art" creates little difficulty. But the elucidation of the evaluative use does. For many, especially theorists, "This is a work of art" does more than describe; it also praises. Its conditions of utterance, therefore, include certain preferred properties or characteristics of art. I shall call these "criteria of evaluation." Consider a typical example of this evaluative use, the view according to which to say of something that it is a work of art is to imply that it is a *successful* harmonization of elements. Many of the honorific definitions of art and its subconcepts are of this form. What is at stake here is that "Art" is construed as an evaluative term which is either identified with its criterion or justified in terms of it. "Art" is defined in terms of its evaluative property, e.g., successful harmonization. On such a view, to say "X is a work of art" is (1) to say something which is taken *to mean* "X is a successful harmonization" (e.g., "Art *is* significant form") or (2) to say something praiseworthy *on the basis* of its successful harmonization. Theorists are never clear whether it is (1) or (2) which is being put forward. Most of them, concerned as they are with this evaluative use, formulate (2), i.e., that feature of art that *makes* it art in the praise-sense, and then go on to state (1), i.e., the definition of "Art" in terms of its art-making feature. And this is clearly to confuse the conditions under which we say something evaluatively with the meaning of what we say. "This is a work of art," said evaluatively, cannot mean "This is a successful harmonization of elements"—except by stipulation—but at most is said in virtue of the art-making property, which is taken as a (the) criterion of "Art," when "Art" is employed to assess. "This is a work of art," used evaluatively, serves to praise and not to affirm the reason why it is said.

The evaluative use of "Art," although distinct from the conditions of its use, relates in a very intimate way to these conditions. For, in every instance of "This is a work of art" (used to praise), what happens is that the criterion of evaluation (e.g., successful harmonization) for the employment of the concept of art is converted into a criterion of recognition. This is why, on its evaluative use, "This is a work of art" implies "This has P," where "P" is some chosen art-making property. Thus, if one chooses to employ "Art" evaluatively, as many do, so that "This is a work of art and not (aesthetically) good" makes no sense, he uses "Art" in such a way that he refuses to *call* anything a work of art unless it embodies his criterion of excellence.

There is nothing wrong with the evaluative use; in fact, there is good reason for using "Art" to praise. But what cannot be maintained is that theories of the evaluative use of "Art" are true and real definitions of the necessary and sufficient properties of art. Instead they are honorific definitions, pure and simple, in which "Art" has been redefined in terms of chosen criteria.

But what makes them—these honorific definitions—so supremely valuable is not their disguised linguistic recommendations; rather it is the *debates* over the reasons for changing the criteria of the concept of art which are built into the definitions. In each of the great theories of art, whether correctly understood as honorific definitions or incorrectly accepted as real definitions, what is of the utmost importance are the reasons profferred in the argument for the respective theory, that is, the reasons given for the chosen or preferred criterion of excellence and evaluation. It is this perennial debate over these criteria of evaluation which makes the history of aesthetic theory the important study it is. The value of each of the theories resides in its attempt to state and to justify certain criteria which are either neglected or distorted by previous theories. Look at the Bell-Fry theory again. Of course, "Art is significant form" cannot be accepted as a true, real definition of art; and most certainly it actually functions in their aesthetics as a redefinition of art in terms of the chosen condition of significant form. But what gives it its aesthetic importance is what lies behind the formula: In an age in which literary and representational elements have become paramount in painting, *return* to the plastic ones since these are indigenous to painting. Thus, the role of the theory is not to define anything but to use the definitional form, almost epigrammatically, to pin-point a crucial recommendation to turn our attention once again to the plastic elements in painting. . . .

Are Art Museums Racist?

Maurice Berger

Walking through a group exhibition installed last fall at the New Museum of Contemporary Art in New York, I heard the distinctive, albeit muffled, voice of the late Malcolm X. The sounds emanated from a multimedium installation by the African-American artist David Hammons. The installation itself, titled *A Fan* (1989), was almost surreal in its juxtapositions: a funeral bouquet, its flowers dried and decayed, stood next to an antique table on which the head of a white, female mannequin "watched"' one of Malcolm X's early television interviews. The work was powerful, challenging, even painful. Rather than advocating conciliation (as he would later), in this video interview Malcolm X spoke of his distrust of white people and of the inherent foolishness of integration. An understandable sense of frustration echoed in his voice when he said, "There is nothing that the white man will do to bring about true, sincere citizenship or civil rights recognition for black people in this country. . . . They will always talk but they won't practice it."

These words offered an appropriate postscript to my museum experience. The exhibition in question was "Strange Attractors: Signs of Chaos," what the curator called an exploration of "some of the most compelling issues raised by the new science of chaos as they relate to recent works of art." The confluence of Malcolm's ideas and the show's theoretical perspective summarized for one the difficult place of African-American artists in museums—even in ones as ostensibly supportive of racial inclusion as the New Museum. The charismatic presence of Malcolm X's voice in "Strange Attractors" simply underscored how irrelevant both the exhibition and its catalogue were to the issues about which he was speaking—that is, when those words could be heard at all, given the video monitor's subdued volume. The catalogue reverberates with the jargon of "the new chaos science": words like *period doubling, bifurcation cascade, phase space, limit cycle, hysteresis* appear throughout its pages. As one reads through the catalogue, one recognizes the names of white, male academics. And while curator Laura Trippi maintains that "the discourse of postmodernism sets up within the aesthetic (sometimes to the point of shrillness) a situation of extreme urgency and indeterminacy," nowhere are the systemic, institutionally defined conditions of racism discussed.

Twenty-five years after Malcolm X was assassinated, "his voice is being heard again and his ideology is being reexamined" as many African-Americans search for new social structures for survival and growth in a period of renewed conservatism and indifference. This search contemplates a radical realignment of society that is

---

An excerpt

unthinkable to most white people—a realignment that is not about chaos but about order. Perhaps it is the urgency of this project that made the inclusion of Malcolm X in this art exhibition so striking. Without the Hammons piece the sensibility of "Strange Attractors" would have been very different, more typical of the splashy group shows of contemporary art that simply ignore the issue of race. That one image threw the entire show into question and pointed up the racial bias of its institutional context. Increasingly, across the country, similar catalysts are inserting painful questions into the heretofore complacent space of exhibition as curators with good intentions attempt to "include" the cultural production of people of color.

Having grown up in a predominantly black and Hispanic low-income housing project on Manhattan's Lower East Side—a place that was presumably also about good intentions—I am used to the experience of witnessing social and cultural indifference to people of color as a white person on the inside. It is startling to me, however, that in a nation that has seen at least some effort made by white people to share mainstream cultural venues (and the concomitant social and economic rewards) with African-Americans and other people of color—most notably in the areas of popular music, dance, literature and theater—the visual arts remain, for the most part, stubbornly resistant. My point in this article, then, is to examine the complex institutional conditions that result in the exclusion or misrepresentation of major cultural voices in the United States. These muted voices are complex and varied. There are veteran black artists, such as Al Loving, Faith Ringgold and the late Romare Bearden, who have received considerable art-world attention but are prevented from rising to the superstar status available to white artists of equal (or less than equal) talent. There are the younger African-American artists of the so-called MFA generation, such as Maren Hassinger, Pat Ward Williams and David Hammons, who have had considerable difficulty finding gallery representation. And finally, there is a new generation of "outsiders," artists and collectives that function independently of the gallery system in communities across the country.

Viewed in the broader context of social changes in American race relations—from the advances of the civil rights movement in the 1960s to the reversal of many of these advances in the Reagan era—the question of black cultural disenfranchisement seems daunting. Is the art world merely mirroring social changes or can art institutions actually play a role in challenging the conditions of institutional racism in America? Sad to say, with regard to race, art museums have for the most part behaved like many other businesses in this country—they have sought to preserve the narrow interests of their upperclass patrons and clientele. It is this upper-class, mostly white bias that I want to interrogate in order to find out "what's going on with whiteness" (as the writer bell hooks might say) at one of America's most racially biased cultural institutions—the art museum.

Despite the recent increase in exhibitions devoted to African-American art in major museums, these shows rarely address the underlying resistance of the art world to people of color. Such exhibitions often fall into what the art historian Judith Wilson has called the syndrome of "separate-but-unequal programming": African-American shows in February, during Black History Month, white shows the rest of the year. A recent study of "art-world racism" in New York from 1980–87 by artist Howardena Pindell seems to verify that white-identified galleries and museums have little interest in enfranchising African-Americans and other people of color. Based on her statistical overview of the demographics of mainstream art exhibitions, Pindell concludes that "black, Hispanic, Asian, and Native American artists are . . . with a few, very few, exceptions systematically excluded.' PESTS, an anonymous group of New York-based African, Asian, Latino and Native American artists organized in 1986 to combat "art-world apartheid," came to a similar conclusion. In 1987, the *PESTS Newsletter* published a roster of 62 top New York galleries whose stables were all or nearly all white. While the situation would appear to be somewhat better outside of New York (a city where, Wilson claims, "the relative economic powerlessness of the black population . . . keeps displays at the . . . largest, publicly funded museums less integrated"), African-American and other artists of color remain underrepresented in museums and galleries across the United States.

During the past 25 years a number of institutions devoted to African-American art and culture have opened in the United States, a response to the general problem of institutional racism and the art world's frustrating indifference to people of color. The Studio Museum in Harlem, for example, was founded in 1967 to fill a void left by mainstream institutions; its mission was to support the "study, documentation, collection, preservation and exhibition of art and artifacts of Black America and the African diaspora." The Studio Museum is to the African-American art world as the Museum of Modern Art is to the white art establishment in terms of visibility and prestige. But there are literally hundreds of smaller, lesser-known institutions across the country devoted to the art of African-Americans and other people of color. Such alternative museums raise a number of questions about the relationship between white and black culture in America. Are African-American artists stifled by the segregation by black museums, or do these institutions allow their art to flourish despite the dominant culture's lack of interest? Must African-Americans renounce their own cultural identity in order to be accepted by mainstream institutions? To what extent does the mere existence of African-American museums unintentionally absolve majority institutions of their social responsibility to black Americans?

Kinshasha Holman Conwill, executive director of the Studio Museum in Harlem, maintains that African-American museums are necessary:

> Black artists are segregated by society. If we waited for Romare Bearden, Al Loving or Betye Saar or other black artists to have their retrospectives at the Museum of Modern Art or in some of the wonderful contemporary museums around this country, we would be waiting a long, long time. Many people ask me if the [Studio Museum] perpetuates [this problem]. It's as if racism would end tomorrow if we disbanded the Studio Museum in Harlem, and there would be this great opening of doors and black artists would start pouring in to the mainstream of American art. Well, that's not what is happening.

On the whole, the financial situation for African-American and other minority art institutions remains poor. The American Association of Museums (AAM) in

Washington, D.C., has begun to address the needs of these institutions, but their own rigorous accreditation standards, including stringent technical and acquisition guidelines, actually discourage validation of younger and economically poorer institutions. The Studio Museum in Harlem, accredited in 1987, is still the only black or Hispanic museum certified by the AAM. Because most corporate and private sponsors insist on proof of accreditation as part of their grant-giving process, lack of accreditation has serious consequences for institutions seeking outside funding. As a result, alternative spaces devoted to African-American art, a relatively recent programming phenomenon, are often dependent on severely limited funding sources. This problem of accreditation is so serious that the Association of African-American Museums was formed recently to help validate institutions overlooked by the AAM. The Ford Foundation, responding to its own study of 29 black and Hispanic art museums, recently instituted a three-year, $5-million program designed to improve economic conditions in these museums. . . .

Still, few programs are directed toward improving African-American representation in white-identified, mainstream art venues. Even fewer programs press the culture industry to examine its own racism and indifference. A rare instance was the program for this year's annual conference of the College Art Association in New York, where an unprecedented number of presentations were devoted to issues of cultural disenfranchisement and institutional racism. Mainstream support of the interests of the "Other" (when it does occur) generally takes one of two forms. By far the more prevalent approach depends on a pragmatic, statistically calibrated inclusion of artists of color, either as tokens in mostly white group shows or, more likely, in token exhibitions devoted exclusively to people of color. This statistical approach is one way of correcting years of exclusion from the art world. Other institutions take a second approach. Wishing to go beyond mere quotas, they organize exhibitions concerned with exploring and ultimately embracing cultural and social differences. The Dallas Museum of Art, for example, has instituted progressive programming in order to confront the reality that "our museums are devoted almost exclusively to the representation of 'white' culture, our libraries to the Western tradition of literature, our universities to the history of ancient Mediterranean and modern Europe." Significantly, the 1987 appointment of Alvia Wardlaw as the DMA's adjunct curator of African-American art made her the first holder of such a position at a major museum.

But in an art world that remains what Judith Wilson has called "one of the last bastions of white supremacy-by-exclusion," most art museums offer little more than lip service to the concept of racial inclusion. Art that demonstrates its "difference" form the mainstream or that challenges dominant values is rarely acceptable to white curators, administrators and patrons. This cultural elite bases its selections on arbitrary, Eurocentric standards of "taste" and "quality"—the code words of racial indifference and exclusion. "Race has become a trope of ultimate, irreducible difference between cultures, linguistic groups, or adherents of specific belief systems which—more often than not—also have fundamentally opposed economic interests," writes Henry Louis Gates, Jr., in an observation that has searing relevance to the art world. "Race is the ultimate trope of difference because it is so very arbitrary in its application."

These tastemakers, in turn, reflect the interests of the ruling caste of cultural institutions. The boards of art museums, publishers of art magazines and books and owners of galleries rarely hire people of color in policy-making positions. Thus, the task of cultural interpretation—even in instances where artists of color are involved—is usually relegated to "people of European descent, as if their perspective was universal." The very ground of art history, in fact, has proven infertile for most African-American students. As Lowery Sims, associate curator of 20th-century art at the Metropolitan Museum of Art, observes:

> Art history was not a career that black middle-class children were taught to aspire to. For one, the Eurocentrism of art history often made it irrelevant to black college students who never heard African-American culture discussed in art-history classes. Museums—the major conduit for teaching young people about art—were not always accessible to blacks. African-Americans were socialized into certain careers after Reconstruction; visual art was not one of them. The economic realities made a career in art even less desirable. You didn't see many black visual artists until the 1920s and '30s, when the black colleges started to establish art departments. Black art historians are an even rarer breed.

While majority museums have not totally ignored the interests of people of color, they have had an extremely difficult time approaching cultures outside of the Anglo-European tradition. The 1969 exhibition "Harlem on My Mind" at the Metropolitan Museum in New York remains the classic example of the deep problems between white institutions and people of color. Twenty years later, the issues surrounding "Harlem on My Mind" offer an interesting model for rethinking our own era of cultural indifference to people of color.

Organized by the white art historian Allon Schoener, then visual-arts director of the New York State Council on the Arts, the exhibition represented an unprecedented effort on the part of an old-line American art museum to sociologically "interpret" African-American culture. The exhibition was not an art show in the traditional sense but an ambitious historical survey of Harlem from 1900 to 1968. Attempting to celebrate Harlem as the "cultural capital of black America," the show consisted of blown-up photographs, photomurals, slide and film projections and audio recordings. As Schoener explained in his introduction to the exhibition's catalogue, the objective of "Harlem on My Mind" was "to demonstrate that the black community in Harlem is a major cultural environment with enormous strength and potential . . . [a] community [that] has made major contributions to the mainstream of American culture in music, theater, and literature." Art was one form of cultural expression not mentioned by Schoener, despite the exhibition's location in a major New York art museum. This omission seemed to reflect Schoener's conviction that "museums should be electronic information centers" and that "paintings have stopped being a vehicle for valid expression in the 20th century." While responding to the ideological inadequacies of elitist art museums, Schoener's view also allowed the Metropolitan to almost completely ignore African-American painting and sculpture. Schoener felt free to construct a sociopolitical profile of Harlem, but he never applied this sociological methodology to his own position or to that of the museum that commissioned him. Rather than engaging Harlem writers, art historians and intellectuals to help interpret the culture of Harlem, a "curious" Schoener felt compelled to conduct his own investigation of the subject because *he* decided "it was time . . . [to find] something out about this other world."

When it opened, the show was widely condemned by African-Americans and others as yet another example of white carpetbagging and well-intentioned meddling. In a 1969 *Artform* critique, historian Eugene Genovese questioned the proliferation of material related to Malcolm X in the exhibition:

> There are pictures of Malcolm the Muslim minister and the street-corner speaker and of Malcolm the corpse, together with indifferent excerpts from his magnificent autobiography. The exhibit immediately involved political decisions: should you emphasize the early or the late Malcolm? Malcolm the uncompromising black nationalist or Malcolm the man who ended his life edging toward a new position? The exhibition settles these questions in a manner that will not be to everyone's taste, but the real problem lies elsewhere: Who is making the decision to interpret Malcolm? Since the show purports to be a cultural history of Harlem, only that community as a whole or, more realistically, one or more of the clearly identified groups recognized as legitimate by the people of Harlem have the right.

Concluding his discussion of Malcolm X, Genovese suggested a compelling metaphor for the problem with "Harlem on My Mind." Trying to listen to Malcolm's speeches in the exhibition galleries, Genovese realized that he could not hear them because "the loudspeaker in one room drown[ed] out the one in the next." As in "Strange Attractors," the voice of one of America's most influential black leaders had been subjugated by the curatorial apparatus of an art exhibition. In each case, the museum's attempt to deal with African-American culture was in the end simply embarrassing. While Malcolm X can be an engaging, even sympathetic figure for white curators, his complex teachings must be understood first of all in relation to the African-American community to whom he was principally speaking. It is not that white people are incapable of analyzing his ideas but rather that cultural interpretations offered in exhibitions like "Harlem on My Mind" and "Strange Attractors" can never stray too far from the interests of their white, upper-class patrons or their principally white audience. . . .

On the Concept of Music

Jerrold Levinson

. . . We should at the outset distinguish the question "What is music?" from some others with which it might be confused. One of these is the question of what *kind* of thing a piece of music is—that is to say, what ontological or metaphysical category (e.g., particular, universal, mental, physical) it belongs to and what its identity conditions are. This question . . . can to a large extent be dealt with independently of the distinction between music and nonmusic, and vice versa. We can determine what it is to count something as an instance or occasion of music without deciding precisely what ontological characterization pieces of music should receive.

A second question is how we generally *recognize* something to be music—what criteria we employ in making judgments of that sort, by ear, in ordinary situations. It should be apparent that this is more a psychological question than a conceptual one. It asks, in effect, for *typical* features of music which are aurally accessible and prominently noted—e.g., regular meter, definite rhythm, melody, harmony. But something might be a piece of music that lacked almost all typical musical features, and might possess many such features without being a piece of music. There are, furthermore, conditions essential to being a piece of music which are not even directly hearable, and which thus cannot figure as criteria of *recognition.* Nor, since our criteria for recognition are fallible, will everything that satisfies them in fact be an instance of music. A third question asks what it is that makes a piece of music *good,* or *great,* or just *better* than some other piece of music. This question is clearly an evaluative one and should be kept separate from the fundamentally descriptive inquiry into the bounds of music per se, as contrasted with nonmusic.

It has often been suggested that music be defined as *organized sound.* But this is patently inadequate. While sonic organization has some plausibility as a necessary feature of music, it is hardly a sufficient one. The output of a jackhammer, the ticking of a metronome, the shouts of a drill sergeant during a march, the chirping of a sparrow, the roar of a lion, the whine of a police siren, a presidential campaign speech—all are organized sounds but not instances of music.

We can prevent the roar of the lion and the chirping of the sparrow from being counted as music if we amend the initial proposal so as to require that the organized sound be *humanly* produced—or at least produced by intelligent creatures to whom we might accord the status of *persons.* For it seems that one would not strictly consider anything music which was not the outcome of intentional activity on the part of an

---

An excerpt

intelligent being. On the other hand, this may just be indicative of a deeper reason for excluding roars and chirps—that they do not exhibit the appropriate aim or purpose for qualifying as music. I will return to this point later.

Even if we introduce "humanly" as a qualification to "organized sound," we are still left with various sonic items mentioned above which conform to this conception but are not indeed instances of music. We might seek to exclude many of these (e.g., the jackhammer output, the presidential speech) by insisting on those features of music which an elementary textbook of music considers definitive (e.g., *melody, rhythm, harmony*). But that this will not do is brought home to us by early music, contemporary music, and music of non-Western cultures. Gregorian chant and shakuhachi solos are music but lack harmony. Takemitsu's *Water Music* (derived from taped raindrop sounds), African drumming, and Webern's pointillistic *Five Pieces,* op. 5, lack melody but are nonetheless music. Certain kinds of atmospheric modern jazz and synthesizer compositions have virtually no rhythms, yet they are music also. Melody, rhythm, and harmony are important features of a lot of music, but they nonetheless remain only typical features for music in general, not necessary ones. In fact, it should be apparent that there are no longer any intrinsic properties of sound that are required for something possibly to be music, and none that absolutely excludes a sonic phenomenon from that category.

It might be thought that what makes African drumming, modern jazz, and Mozart piano concertos music is that they are all organizations of sound which stir the soul or, more soberly, affect the *emotions.* Or perhaps ones that express the emotions of their *creators.* But although emotional evocation and emotional expression are central aspects of most music, they are not definitive ones. The roar of the lion and the whine of the police siren induce emotion in the auditor perhaps more surely than most music does. The orator's speech and the poet's lyric (possibly also the lion's roar) may express their creators' emotions as much as does the *Pathétique* Sonata. On the other hand, some music seems neither the embodiment of a creator's inner state nor a stimulus to emotional response in hearers, but rather an abstract configuration of sounds in motion and/or a reflection of some nonindividual—or even nonhuman—aspect of things. Examples of this might be some Javanese gamelan music, Bach's *Art of the Fugue,* George Crumb's *Makrokosmos,* Conlon Nancarrow's *Studies for Player Piano,* and Tibetan ritual music. So it is clear that music cannot be defined by some special relation to emotional life; no such relation holds for *all* music and *only* for music. Nor can music be understood as humanly organized sound that transmits or communicates *ideas* or the like. For this net is far too wide. Though it may include much music, it also includes sirens, shouts, and messages in Morse code.

It should be fairly obvious that what our preliminary definition lacks, and what is needed to get close to the concept of music, is some sufficiently general notion of the *aim* or *purpose* for which the humanly organized sound in question is produced. Music is such sounds produced (or determined) with a certain *intent.* But what intent is this? Since music in the primary sense is an art (or artistic activity), and the arts are doubtless the foremost arena for aesthetic appreciation, it might seem that music could be defined as "humanly organized sound for the purpose of *aesthetic appreciation.*"

Indeed, this is an advance over "organized sound," but there are significant flaws in this formulation which prevent us from resting with it as an acceptable definition.

One flaw is that there are musics in the world which do not seem aimed at what we can comfortably call "aesthetic appreciation." Music for the accompaniment of ritual, music for the intensification of warlike spirit, and music for dancing are all examples of musics whose proper appreciation does not involve contemplative and distanced apprehension of pure patterns of sound, or put otherwise, does not call for specific attention to its beauty or other aesthetic qualities. Another, perhaps more serious, flaw is the failure of the definition to exclude verbal arts such as drama and (especially) poetry. For poetry, at least in its spoken guise, consists of humanly organized sounds for aesthetic appreciation; it so happens that in that case the sounds are words meaningfully arranged.

We can deal with the poetry problem by requiring that the organized sounds in music be intended for listening to primarily *as sounds,* and not primarily as symbols of discursive thought. This is not to say that music cannot contain words—clearly songs, opera, *musique concrète,* and collage musics do—only that to constitute music the verbal component must either be combined with more purely sonorous material or, if not so accompanied, be such that one is to attend to it primarily for its sonic qualities and whatever is supervenient on them.

The other difficulty is that regarding the ultimate *end* of attending to organized sound as sound. We need to find a replacement for "aesthetic appreciation," since this is too narrow an end to comprise all activity that we would count as the making of music. One suggestion would be this: that music, whether absorbed reflectively in a concert hall or reacted to frenetically during a village rite, is engaged in so that a certain *heightening* of life, or of consciousness, is attained. In other words, all sound phenomena that are categorizable as music seem aimed at the *enrichment or intensification of experience* via engagement with organized sounds as such. I claim that this is indeed the central core of the music-making intention. It is this that enables us to construe examples from any number of times and places as examples of the artistic-cultural activity we conceive of as music, despite the absence of any limiting intrinsic sonic characteristics beyond that of mere audibility.

An instructive hypothetical example that we would not count as music, and which our definition in its present state just manages to exclude, is the following. Imagine a sequence of sounds devised by a team of psychological researchers which are such that when subjects are in a semiconscious condition and are exposed to these sounds, the subjects enter psychedelic states of marked pleasurability. Such a sequence is not a piece of music; yet it is humanly organized sound for the purpose (arguably) of enriching experience. It does not, however, seek this enrichment through requiring a person's *attention* to the sounds as such. Sound organized for our own good but which does not ask us to listen to or otherwise actively engage with it is not music.

Now that our definition is approaching adequacy we must add one minor qualification, making explicit something only implicit until now: namely, that the organization of sound must be *temporal* organization if the product is to count as musical. What other sort of organization could there be? Well, one can imagine an art in which the point was to produce colorful instantaneous combinations of sounds—i.e., chords of vanishingly brief duration—which were to be savored independently, each in splendid isolation from the next. My intuition is that we would not regard this art as a type of music (though existing musical knowledge and technique would be relevant to its successful practice). It would be the auditory equivalent of jam tasting or rose smelling—the receiving of a sensory impression, sometimes complex, but one for which temporal development was not an issue. Music as we conceive it seems as essentially an art of time as it is an art of sound.

Our complete definition of music would then go roughly like this:

> *Music* = df sounds temporarily organized by a person for the purpose of enriching or intensifying experience through active engagement (e.g., listening, dancing, performing) with the sounds regarded primarily, or in significant measure as sounds.

I believe this formulation covers all that it should—e.g., classical music, folk music, party music, avant-garde music, opera, the varied phenomena studied by ethnomusicologists—and nothing it should not (including Muzak).

Some brief observations on the analysis, highlighting its salient features: (1) The analysis accords to music certain intrinsic characteristics, albeit limited ones—to wit, soundingness or audibility, and temporal structure. (2) The analysis is intentionalistic and human-centered; it is people (or the near like) who make music in a purposive way, and not unthinking Nature. (3) The analysis purports to be adequate in application cross-culturally, though of course it is not intended as an analysis of any other culture's concept. (4) The analysis explicitly ascribes a normative attitude to the makers or offerers of music: they necessarily conceive or intend their efforts as worth interacting with. (5) The analysis is creator-oriented or creator-driven: producers make their production music, through their intentional orientation in bringing it forth, and not the receivers or consumers of such production through anything they might do. . . . I now raise [a further point] about the concept of music. The first is that there is a distinction between what *is* music, and what can be *treated* or *regarded* as music. One way to ignore this distinction is to claim, in the spirit of John Cage's Zen-inspired reflections, that any and all sounds are music. This is simply false, and the most cogent of Cage's reflections fails to establish it. What Cage shows perhaps is that any sounds can be listened to *as if* they were music (i.e., attentively, with regard to form, with emotional sensitivity), that one can transform (just about) any sonic environment into an occasion for receptive awareness. It does not follow that all sound events are at present music. The whirr of my blender and the whistling of the wind are not instances of music. They could only be such if they were produced, or proffered, for a certain purpose, as indicated above. But one can *adopt* attitudes toward them which are appropriate for music, with varying degrees of reward.

This Cagean view of music connects to a use of "music" with some currency, in which the word serves as in effect a predicate of experience. The rule of usage is roughly this. If there is a musical experience going on—characterized in some phenomenological fashion or other—then there is music; if not, then the situation is devoid of music. The auditor, through having the right kind of experience, determines whether music is present or is occurring; the source of the sounds experienced in the appropriate way, their raison d'être—or even whether they actually exist—is regarded as irrelevant. It should be clear that from my perspective this is a degenerate notion of music, which obscures more than it illuminates, and denies to music several features that I have argued are central to it, namely, sentient origin, artistic intent, and public character. Furthermore, it is a hopelessly relativistic notion, making the status of anything as music (even Mozart piano concertos) relative to each individual listener and occasion. The concepts of a distinctive musical *experience,* or of the hearing of something *as* music, are useful ones, to be sure, but there is little to be gained by collapsing them into the cultural and objective category of music itself. . . .

Virtual Space

Suzanne Langer

. . . In the realm of sculpture the role of illusion seems less important than in painting, where a flat surface "creates" a three-dimensional space that is obviously virtual. Sculpture is actually three-dimensional; in what sense does it "create" space for the eye? This is probably the question which led Hildebrand to say that the sculptor's task was to present a three-dimensional object in the two-dimensional picture place of "perceptual space." But the answer, though it satisfies and, in fact, aptly completes his theory, lacks the confirmation of direct experience and artistic intuition. Sculptors themselves rarely think in terms of pictures, and of ideal planes of vision staggered one behind the other to define deep space (except in perfectly flat relief with rectangular cuts, or even mere graven lines, which is really pictorial art, substituting the graving tool for a pencil). Sculpture, even when it is wedded to a background as in true relief, is essentially *volume,* not *scene.*

The volume, however, is not a cubic measure, like the space in a box. It is more than the bulk of the figure; it is a space made visible, and is more than the area which the figure actually occupies. The tangible form has a complement of empty space that it absolutely commands, that is given with it and only with it, and is, in fact, part of the sculptural volume. The figure itself seems to have a sort of continuity with the emptiness around it, however much its solid masses may assert themselves as such. The void enfolds it, and the enfolding space has vital form as a continuation of the figure. . . .

An excerpt

Here we have the primary illusion, virtual space, created in a mode quite different from that of painting, which is *scene,* the field of direct vision. Sculpture creates an equally visual space, but not a space of direct vision; for volume is really given originally to touch, both haptic touch and contact limiting bodily movement, and the business of sculpture is to translate its data into entirely visual terms, i.e. *to make tactual space visible.*

The intimate relationship between touch and sight which is thus effected by the semblance of kinetic volume explains some of the complex sensory reactions which sculptors as well as laymen often have toward it. Many people feel a strong desire to handle every figure. In some persons the wish springs from obviously sentimental motives, anthropomorphizing the statue, imagining a human contact; this was the attitude Rodin expressed, and the knowledge that he would touch cold marble made him wistful, like Pygmalion. But others—among artists, probably the majority—imagine the touch of stone or wood, metal or earth; they wish to feel the substance that is really there, and let their hands pass over its pure form. They know that the sensation will not always bear out the visual suggestion, perhaps will even contradict it. Yet they believe that their perception of the work will somehow be enhanced.

Sculptural form is a powerful abstraction from actual objects and the three-dimensional space which we construe by means of them, through touch and sight. It makes its own construction in three dimensions, namely the *semblance* of kinetic space. Just as one's field of direct vision is organized, in actuality, as a plane at the distance of a natural focus, so the kinetic realm of tangible volumes, or things, and free air spaces between them, is organized in each person's actual experience as his *environment,* i.e. a space whereof he is the center; his body and the range of its free motion, its breathing space and the reach of its limbs, are his own kinetic volume, the point of orientation from which he plots the world of tangible reality—objects, distances, motions, shape and size and mass. . . .

A piece of sculpture is a center of three-dimensional space. It is a virtual kinetic volume, which dominates a surrounding space, and this environment derives all proportions and relations from it, as the actual environment does from one's self. The work is the semblance of a self, and creates the semblance of a tactual space—and, moreover, a visual semblance. It effects the objectification of self and environment for the sense of sight. Sculpture is literally the image of kinetic volume in sensory space.

That is why I say it is a powerful abstraction. And here I have to depart from [Bruno] Adriani; for he, still speaking of the sculptor, continues: "The space of his [Bruno] sculpture is his original world. . . . The 'ideal' beholder . . . transposes the system of coördinated axes, created by the sculptor, into his own organism." On the contrary, it seems to me that just because we do *not* identify the space which centers in a statue with our own environment, the created world remains objective, and can thus become an *image* of our own surrounding space. It is an environment, but not our own; neither is it that of some other person, having points in common with ours, so that the person and his surroundings become 'objects' to us, existing in our space. Though a statue is, actually, an object, we do not treat it as such; we see it as a center of a space all its own; but its kinetic volume and the environment it creates are illusory—they exist for our vision alone, a semblance of the self and its world.

This explains, perhaps, why the tactual encounter with stone or wood, contradicting as it does the organic appearance of sculpture, may nevertheless cause no disappointment, but may really enhance our appreciation of plastic form; it checks the anthropomorphic fancy, and heightens the abstractive power of the work. Yet handling a figure, no matter what it gives us, is always a mere interlude in our perception of the form. We have to step back, and see it unmolested by our hands, that break into the sphere of its spatial influence. . . .

There is a third mode of creating virtual space, more subtle than the construction of illusory scene or even illusory organism, yet just as commandingly artistic, and in its scope the most ambitious of all; that is architecture. Its "illusion" is easily missed because of the obviousness and importance of its actual values: shelter, comfort, safekeeping. Its practical functions are so essential that architects themselves are often confused about its status. Some have regarded it as chiefly utilitarian, and only incidentally aesthetic, except in the case of monuments; others have treated it as "applied art," wherein practical considerations always force some sacrifice of the artist's "vision"; and some have tried to meet the prosaic demands of utility by making function paramount, believing that genuinely appropriate forms are always beautiful. In architecture the problem of appearance and reality comes to a head as in no other art. This makes it a test case in aesthetic theory, for a true general theory has no exceptions, and when it seems to have them it is not properly stated. If architecture is utilitarian *except* in the case of monuments, then utility is not its essence; if it may be treated as sculpture *except* where practical needs interfere as in underground building, or necessities like bulkheads and chicken houses, then sculptural values are not essential to it. If functional interests can ever be adequately served without beauty, then form may follow function with all the happy effect in the world, but functionality is not the measure of beauty. . . .

As *scene* is the basic abstraction of pictorial art, and *kinetic volume* of sculpture, that of architecture is *an ethnic domain.* Actually, of course, a domain is not a "thing" among other "things"; it is the sphere of influence of a function, or functions; it may have physical effects on some geographical locality or it may not. Nomadic cultures, or cultural phenomena like the seafaring life, do not inscribe themselves on any fixed place on earth. Yet a ship, constantly changing its location, is none the less a self-contained place, and so is a Gypsy camp, an Indian camp, or a circus camp, however often it shifts its geodetic bearings. Literally, we say the camp is *in* a place; culturally, it *is* a place. A Gypsy camp is a different place from an Indian camp, though it may be geographically where the Indian camp used to be.

A place, in this non-geographical sense, is a created thing, an ethnic domain made visible, tangible, sensible. As such it is, of course, an illusion. Like any other plastic symbol, it is primarily an illusion of self-contained, self-sufficient, perceptual space. But the principle of organization is its own: for it is organized as a functional realm made visible—the center of a virtual world, the "ethnic domain," and itself a geographical semblance.

Painting creates planes of vision, or "scene" confronting our eyes, on an actual, two-dimensional surface; sculpture makes virtual "kinetic volume" out of actual three-dimensional material, i.e. actual volume; architecture articulates the "ethnic domain," or virtual "place," by treatment of an actual place.

The architectural illusion may be established by a mere array of upright stones defining the magic circle that severs holiness from the profane, even by a single stone that marks a center, i.e. a monument. The outside world, even though not physically shut out, is dominated by the sanctum and becomes its visible context; the horizon, its frame. The Temple of Poseidon at Sounion shows this organizing power of a composed form. On the other hand, a tomb carved out of solid rock may create a complete domain, a world of the dead. It has no outside; its proportions are internally derived—from the stone, from the burial—and define an architectural space that may be deep and high and wide, within but a few cubits of actual measure. The created "place" is essentially a semblance, and whatever effects that semblance is architecturally relevant. . . .

A culture is made up, factually, of the activities of human being; it is a system of interlocking and intersecting actions, a continuous functional pattern. As such it is, of course, intangible and invisible. It has physical ingredients—artifacts; also physical symptoms—the ethnic effects that are stamped on the human face, known as its "expression," and the influence of social condition on the development, posture, and movement of the human body. But all such items are fragments that "mean" the total pattern of life only to those who are acquainted with it and may be reminded of it. They are ingredients in a culture, not its image.

The architect creates its image: a physically present human environment that expresses the characteristic rhythmic functional patterns which constitute a culture. Such patterns are the alternations of sleep and waking, venture and safety, emotion and calm, austerity and abandon; the tempo, and the smoothness or abruptness of life; the simple forms of childhood and the complexities of full moral stature, the sacramental and the capricious moods that mark a social order, and that are repeated, though with characteristic selection, by every personal life springing from that order. . . .

The most familiar product of architecture is, of course, the *house.* Because of its ubiquity it is the most detailed, and yet the most variable general form. It may shelter one person or a hundred families; it may be made of stone or wood, clay, cement or metal, or many materials together—even paper, grass, or snow. People have made houses in the caves of barren mountains, and houses out of animal skins to take along on the march; they have used spreading trees for roofs, anchoring their houses to the live trunks. The imperative need of dwellings under all conditions, from the polar ice, almost as dead as the moon, to the prodigal Mediterranean lands, has caused every means of construction to be exploited; the house has been the builder's elementary school.

But the great architectural ideas have rarely, if ever, arisen from domestic needs. They grew as the temple, the tomb, the fortress, the hall, the theatre. The reason is simple enough: tribal culture is collective, and its domain therefore essentially public. When it is made visible, its image is a public realm. Most early architecture—Stonehenge, the Mounds, the Temple of the Sun—defines what might be called "religious space." This is a virtual realm; the temple, though oriented by the equinox points, merely symbolizes the "corners of the earth" to simple people who probably did not understand the astronomical scheme at all. The temple really made their greater world of space—nature, the abode of gods and ghosts. The heavenly bodies could be seen to rise and set in the frame it defined; and as it presented this space to popular thought it unified the earth and heaven, men and gods. . . .

In that false assumption lies the error of "functionalism"—lies not very deep, but perhaps as deep as the theory itself goes. Symbolic expression is something miles removed from provident planning or good arrangement. It does not suggest things to do, but embodies the feeling, the rhythm, the passion or sobriety, frivolity or fear with which any things at all are done. That is the image of life which is created in buildings; it is the visible semblance of an "ethnic domain," the symbol of humanity to be found in the strength and interplay of forms. . . .

The most interesting result of the theory, however, is the light it throws on the relation of architecture to sculpture. . . .

The two art forms are, in fact, each other's exact complements: the one, an illusion of kinetic volume, symbolizing the Self, or center of life—the other, an illusion of ethnic domain, or the environment created by Self-hood. Each articulates one half of the life-symbol directly and the other by implication; whichever we start with, the other is its background. . . .

Architecture as Decorated Shelter

Robert Venturi

One way to talk about architecture and analyze where you are in it is to define it. Every architect works with a definition in mind even if he or she doesn't know it, or if it is not explicit; every generation of architects has its own definitions. Our current definition is, architecture is shelter with symbols on it. Or, architecture is shelter with decoration on it.

For many architects this may be a shocking definition because definitions in the last seventy-five years have been put in spatial, technological, organic, or linguistic terms. Definitions of Modern architecture never included ornament, nor did they explicitly refer to shelter. Space and process were the essential qualities of architecture in Louis Kahn's definition, "architecture is the thoughtful making of spaces," and in descriptive phrases like Sigfried Giedion's "space-time and architecture," and Frank Lloyd Wright's "in the nature of materials"; space and form predominated in Le Corbusier's "architecture is the masterly, correct, and magnificent play of masses brought together in light." In his definition of a house as a machine for living in, technology and functionalism were the essential elements, although the implication of functionalism in this famous pronouncement is almost unique in Modern architecture despite the emphasis on functionalism in the general theory of the movement. And recently some theorists have attempted semiotic interpretations of architecture, applying in very literal terms some of the complex techniques of that verbal discipline to the perception of architecture. But ornament and symbolism—certainly applied ornament and the simple uses of association—have been ignored in architecture, or condemned. Ornament as equated with crime by Adolf Loos as long ago as 1906, and symbolism was associated with discredited historical eclecticism; appliqué on shelter would have been considered superficial by theorists of the Modern movement and contrary to the industrial techniques integral to Modern architecture.

But we like emphasizing shelter in architecture, thereby including function in our definition; and we like admitting symbolic rhetoric in our definition which is not integral with shelter, thereby expanding the content of architecture beyond itself and freeing function to take care of itself.

To justify our definition of architecture and to clarify how we come to it, I shall use six comparisons—those between Rome and Las Vegas, Abstract Expressionism and Pop Art, Vitruvius and Gropius, Mies van der Rohe and McDonald's hamburger stands, Scarlatti and the Beatles, and plain and fancy styles of architecture. In the last three comparisons I shall try to justify a particular content for symbolism in architecture, that of the ordinary. For my arguments I shall use material from our book, *Learning from Las Vegas,* because I am elaborating here on a main theme in that book, and because I think hardly anyone has read that book or reads books in general anymore.

ROME AND LAS VEGAS

As architects, we appreciate Rome *and* Las Vegas and we have learned from both sources. (I use Rome to stand for urban tradition—Medieval and Baroque—and Las Vegas to stand for urban sprawl in general.) It is in comparisons between the Roman piazza and the Vegas Strip—illustrating surprising similarities as well as obvious contrasts—that we learned about symbolism in architecture.

Our generation discovered Rome in the fifties. Enclosed exterior space and intimate urban scale were exciting revelations to those of us growing up along wide, ill-defined streets and vast parking lots in amorphous (although not yet hostile) American cities. As post-heroic Moderns reading Sigfried Giedion, we rediscovered history and acknowledged a traditional basis for architecture and urbanism. We had a particular sympathy for the spatial relationships, pedestrian scale, and urban quality of Italian towns exemplified in the piazza. We are now suffering from the results of that enthusiasm—witness the subsequent urban renewal piazzas that disrupt the social fabric and dry up the commercial and visual vitality of the centers of American cities. This is because, as architects of the fifties, we saw the piazza as pure space and we designed our piazzas as dry configurations of compositional elements—forms and textures, patterns and colors, rhythms, accents, and scale—balanced somehow to promote urbanity in space. Historical urban complexes we saw as abstract compositions like those of the Abstract Expressionist paintings of that decade: the symbolism of the building in the piazzas we hardly saw at all. We appreciated the rich evolutionary juxtapositions of historical styles—Baroque palazzo facing Romanesque duomo, for instance—but we limited our observations to the formal relationships of these styles. We ignored the symbolic content of the buildings because of our obsession with the composition of space. We forgot that forms were buildings, texture was sculptural relief, an accent was a statue (and a statue represented a person and ideals), articulation was a portal or decoration, rhythm was composed of pilasters, color and pattern were functions of walls, and that a focus was an obelisk—a sign commemorating an important event. We blotted out the explicit associations evoked by most of the architectural and sculptural elements of the piazza; the ornamentation on the facade of the palazzo symbolizing architectural and structural content and promoting dynastic virtues and civic values, and that of the cathedral, which is like a complex billboard with niches for saintly icons.

We ignored iconography in architecture when we stressed the functional and structural qualities of building in piazzas and idolized their spatial effects, but forgot their symbolic dimensions. We learned inspiring lessons about space in Rome, but the urbanity we were seeking would come from space and signs. We had to go to Las Vegas to learn this lesson about Rome and to acknowledge symbolism in our definition of architecture. On the other hand, we were able to be easy and perceptive about Las Vegas in the sixties because we loved Rome in the fifties.

We had an exhilarating feeling of revelation in Las Vegas in the sixties, like that which we had in Rome in the previous decade. Our first reaction was that the Strip has a quality and a vitality—a significance—that Modern-designed urban landscapes don't have, and that, ironically, where Modern architecture had won out by supposedly bringing urbanity back to our cities, it didn't. When we analyzed our happy reaction and the peculiar quality and adhesion that exists in commercial urban sprawl, we found that their basis was symbolism. As we had learned from the spaces of Rome, we learned from the symbolism of Las Vegas. We soon learned that if you ignore signs as "visual pollution," you are lost. If you look for "spaces between buildings" in Las Vegas, you are lost. If you see the buildings of urban sprawl as forms making space, they are pathetic—mere pimples in an amorphous landscape. As architecture, urban sprawl is a failure; as space, it is nothing. It is when you see the buildings as symbols in space, not forms in space, that the landscape takes on quality and meaning. And when you see no buildings at all, at night when virtually only the illuminated signs are visible, you see the Strip in its pure state.

This is not to say that the architecture I am describing is without formal content, but to emphasize the predominance of signs over buildings on the Strip and of symbolism over form in the buildings on the Strip as functions of the vast spaces they are seen in and the fast speeds they are seen at. We enumerated, in *Learning from Las Vegas,* the uses of mixed media in architecture, including bold representational kinds of architecture, to create impact and identity—indeed, to be perceived at all—from highways and over parking lots, day and night. In the landscape of the auto age a picture is worth a thousand forms.

In that book we concentrated on the techniques rather than the content of commercial vernacular architecture to help us learn how to design our own architecture. In learning from Las Vegas in this way we were not promoting manipulative giant corporatism or even acquiescing to it, as many of our critics—usually architects of the political left in Europe and those of the aesthetic right in the United States—would have it, any more than our Modern architectural grandfathers promoted exploitative free-market capitalism in learning from the industrial vernacular of their day, or than the same critics, if analyzing Versailles or il Gesú, would be advocating a return to absolutism or the Counter-Reformation. Separating technique from content is a traditional and still useful method of analysis and criticism of old or new art, high or low design.

The content of the symbolism of commercial sprawl is different from that of the traditional city, but the commercial messages of the Strip, although bolder to suit our coarser sensibilities and the more gross tempos of our time, are hardly more promotional than the messages on the palaces and cathedral in the piazza promoting civic and religious ideals and power, when you understand the iconography of these forms. Nor is the popular art of the Strip necessarily more promotional than the high design of the "masterly, correct, and magnificent play of masses" of the corporate headquarters, now that big business has taken over the "progressive" symbolism of orthodox Modern architecture. We ourselves often feel less uncomfortable with the crass commercial advertising on the roadside than we do with some of the subtle and tasteful persuasion inherent in the Modern formalist symbolism that pervades corporate architecture, including that of the industrial-military complex. We think that the sources of many of the visual problems of the roadside commercial environment are more economic, social, and cultural than aesthetic—stemming from the low economic status of some roadside communities, from the bad habits of Americans prone to littering and to "public squalor," and from the varying taste cultures of a multiethnic, heterogeneous society.

ABSTRACT EXPRESSIONISM AND POP ART

Pop Art in the sixties turned our sensibilities toward the commercial Strip as the painting of the decade before it confirmed our interpretation of the piazza. I have explained how we looked at the piazza in that decade in the same way that we looked at an Abstract Expressionist painting, and how this limited our vision of the urban landscape. The Pop artists opened up our eyes and our minds by showing us again the value of representation in painting, and bringing us thereby to association as an element of architecture. They also showed us the value of familiar and conventional elements by juxtaposing them in new contexts in different scales to achieve new meanings perceived along with their old meanings. Definitions of architecture now included meaning via association as well as expression—a term of the fifties—via perception. And these artists held, we realized later, an ironic view in their love-hate relationship with their vulgar commercial subject matter, paralleling ours toward our ordinary commercial architecture; they made seeing Las Vegas easier, while being still a little uneasy. And now the photorealists of the seventies, whose subject matter is the urban landscape, paint Las Vegas, enhancing the ordinary and beautifying the spectacular.

VITRUVIUS AND GROPIUS

My third comparison, in my attempt to justify architecture as the decoration of shelter, is between Vitruvius and Gropius. (I use the proper noun Gropius in this comparison to stand for orthodox Modern architecture in general and because of its alliteration.) You will recall the traditional Vitruvian definition of architecture in the words of Sir Henry Wooton: Architecture is firmness, commodity, and delight. The twentieth-century paraphrase of this definition might be: Architecture is structure, program, and expression. (Jean Labatut used to add: shake well before using.) Orthodox Modern architects, if not Walter Gropius then his followers, would significantly alter the Vitruvian juxtaposition of elements. Using the same words, they would have said: Structure and program *are* architecture. When you get structure and program right, expressive architecture will be the automatic result. You shouldn't try for beauty, if you would, indeed, mention that word; architectural quality; the spatial and expressive quality of a building, comes out of the harmonious solution of structural and functional problems. Architecture became frozen process. Certainly the aesthetic element in a Virtuvian triad could not derive from appliqué ornament or from symbolism. Architecture could not represent beauty, it could only be.

It is obvious there is no ornament on Gropius's building of the mid-twenties for the Bauhaus in Dessau, but it is hard to believe its form is merely a result of process—of, as Gropius claimed, "our advance from the vagaries of mere architectural caprice to the dictates of structural logic." This building is really a sensitive and effective reworking of an industrial architectural vocabulary of steel frame, glass walls, and flowing space, an adaptation of an existing industrial vernacular architecture of simple geometric forms. It is, indeed, a symbolic building, symbolic of industrial process and advanced technology, whose effect derives in part from the affective properties of its industrial forms. Gropius was doing something different from what he said. There is nothing wrong with this because architects' theories and work often don't correspond; the important thing is that the work be effective. But it is significant, I think, that although Gropius vehemently denied that the Bauhaus could "propagate any 'style,' system, dogma, formula, or vogue," and claimed "a 'Bauhaus Style' would have been a confession of failure and a return to that very stagnation and devitalizing inertia which I had called it into being to combat," he did what architects and artists inevitably do. They intuitively choose a formal vocabulary, an order, a system, a convention, and then adapt it (sometimes avowedly) to their own uses. The Modern movement, whatever was said, picked an existing vocabulary of forms, as the Renaissance master chose the Classical Roman orders, and as we are contemplating the contemporary commercial vernacular.

Of course there were other sources for the forms and symbols of Modern architecture of the heroic period, derived from fine art as well as vernacular art, Cubist painting being an obvious one. Le Corbusier, almost uniquely among the theorists of the Modern movement, admitted to his formalistic adaptation of Cubism and existing mechanical and industrial forms. He was frankly enamored of midwestern American grain elevators which he illustrated in *Towards a New Architecture* in the twenties, he painted Cubist compositions and liked steamships and automobiles. He also illustrated the early Christian basilica of S. Maria in Cosmedin in Rome, focusing on the severe, white, almost Cubist marble furniture in the sanctuary. It is significant that Le Corbusier's architecture of that period looked more like the midwestern grain elevators, steamships, and automobiles illustrated in his book than like the altar of S. Maria in Cosmedin. Why? Because S. Maria was symbolically wrong if formally right, whereas the other precedents were formally and symbolically appropriate. Le Corbusier admittedly employed a formal vocabulary that he adapted and used symbolically to a significant degree, taking existing forms and changing their context. Despite the revolutionary rhetoric of his words, association relying on past experience was part of his architecture.

The main trouble with rejecting a formal system in architecture is that the architects who do so in order to avoid the dangers of formalism, ironically, become more prone to formalism. Late-Modern fundamentalist architects accepted the words of the artists of the heroic period but not the substance of their work. By attempting to exclude symbolism and decoration, and by emphasizing spatial and structural expression, they ended with an architecture of abstract expressionism: pure but limited, it was soon not enough. So they substituted articulation for decoration—articulation through the exaggeration of structural and functional elements: structure protrudes rhythmically, functions protrude sensitively, clerestories pulsate on the roof. Articulation provides visual richness for form stripped of decoration. In frequent cases, orgies of complex and contradictory articulations produce dramatic expression that becomes expressionism in architecture. Ironically, the exclusion of applied ornament distorts the whole building into *an* ornament. The result is fundamentally more irresponsible than an appliqué of ornament over unarticulated forms would be. We feel that ours is not an era for expressive form and architectural space, but for flat manifestations of symbolism in the landscape—not for the Gallerie des Machines, but for S. Maria in Cosmedin and for the frescoes that were originally applied all over it inside.

There are architects currently working who adopt forms eclectically rather than distort forms expressionistically, but these architects still shun ornamental appliqué. I refer to how the New York Five, sometimes known as the Whites, employ symbolism by quite literally adopting the forms of Le Corbusier's houses of the twenties, and those of De Stijl. Our argument with them is their choice of symbolism: are Cubist industrial forms interesting or relevant for an eclectic style now? Certainly the rather dry abstractions of the houses of the New York Five lack the tension and complexity that was essential to the original houses. We enjoy the unintended irony, however, that these houses are little different in manner from the copies of Norman manor houses and eighteenth-century farmhouses which traditional architects were designing in the twenties and which Le Corbusier and his followers were reacting against at that time. The Italian Rationalists, like the New York Five, are adopting a particular historical style which is minus ornament, and in our context, full of irony; they are a proclaimed Communist-architectural group who are adopting the monumental forms of the Modern, as opposed to the historical-traditional branch of the Italian Fascist style of the twenties and thirties, with meager rationalization on their part for their rather de Chirico images.

Neither the expressionistic nor the eclectic approaches described above leaves much room for function. It seems that in the end pure functionalism in architecture has been deflected toward something more decorative where function is distorted for the sake of functionalist-structuralist styling or ignored as it is abstracted into pure symbolism. The definition of architecture as shelter with symbols on it presupposes an acceptance of the functional doctrine, not a rejection of it—an augmentation of it for the sake of maintaining it. Why not admit the impossibility of maintaining pure functionalism in architecture and the almost inevitable contradictions between functional and aesthetic requirements in the same building, and then let function and decoration go their own separate ways so that functional requirements need not be distorted for unadmitted decorative aims.

MIES VAN DER ROHE AND MCDONALD'S HAMBURGER STANDS

Our fourth comparison, between Mies van der Rohe and McDonald's hamburger stands, is to justify a particular kind of symbolism in architecture. We refer to Mies's work here as representative of the best in Modern architecture and to remind ourselves that Modern architecture went to the industrial vernacular for inspiration for its forms. Mies's work, after he came to the United States, is an even more literal adaptation of an industrial vernacular than Gropius's or Le Corbusier's. His almost Classical orders, derived from the exposed steel I-beams of a certain kind of American factory, were applied, as is well known, with artful contortion, almost as pilasters, to symbolize industrial process and pure order and yet to conform to acceptable standards of fire protection for nonindustrial buildings.

A "factory" of Mies's is vernacular art enhanced as fine art; a McDonald's on the strip is folk art derived from fine art. The history of art reveals many evolutions between low art and high art, back and forth: third movement themes in the sonata form are scherzo folk tunes, plastic madonnas are Baroque survivals. The parabolic arches of a McDonald's pavilion—illuminated yellow plastic—produce a bold and picturesque image, an effective gestalt from the context of a car driving down the strip, but in the mind they symbolize advanced engineering and good eats.

I refer to the classic version of the pavilion with "structural" arches, rather than the tasteful version with mansard roof, current in our era of roadside beautification. But the iconographic evolution of the McDonald's arch is complex. In its original version it is perhaps derived from Le Corbusier's project, in the twenties, for the Palace of the Soviets, where the arch, in contrast to those of McDonald's, actually supports the roof by cables, and from Eero Saarinen's St. Louis arch, itself a symbol for the "gateway to the West." An original manifestation of the parabolic arch was Eugène Freyssinet's hangars at Orly—an almost pure engineering solution for spanning a great distance at a great height to economically house big dirigibles—whose form made a great impression on Modern architects. The final manifestation of the parabolic arch in these evolutions between high art and low art, form and symbol, and among engineering, architecture, and sculpture, is a commercial sign—the reincarnation of two parabolic arches as siamese twins and a letter of the alphabet—the Big M.

To say that a factory is beautiful was shocking fifty years ago. Since then the paintings of Sheeler and Leger, the cover of *Fortune* magazine, the whole repertory and literature of Modern architecture and sculpture have made industrial forms easy to like. But the shock value of this revelation was of tremendous importance at the time. The history of art contains many examples of shock treatment as an aid to the understanding of art. *Épater le bourgeoisie* is a constant theme in the thinking, theorizing, and practice of Modern painters of the nineteenth century. The introduction of pagan Classical orders in fifteenth-century Florence must have had an effect on late Medieval critics akin to the indignation aroused among our orthodox critics by the "crass materialism of our mass society" represented in the commercial vernacular architecture we are looking at now. This kind of outrage does not apply to the exploitative labor practices associated with the beautiful cast-iron fronts of early capitalist loft buildings nor to the harsh realities behind the crafted forms and symbols of primitive villages so admired by the same critics today. And these latter-day Moderns fail to see the ironic parallel between their outrage over the commercial vernacular and that of their Beaux-Arts predecessors over the industrial vernacular as a source for fine art fifty years ago. There was shock value in the Romantic discovery of the natural landscape—of daffodils in fields as a fit subject for poetry, and of peasant architecture—in the Hameau off the allée at Versailles, as there was in the transposition of common speech in the prose and poetry of James Joyce and T. S. Eliot. Returning to the ordinary, looking at the existing again, enhancing the conventional, are old ways of making new art.

My second comparison illustrated the affinity of late Modern architecture to the Abstract Expressionism of the fifties. This fourth comparison connects with the 1850s which were the heyday of the Industrial Revolution. Although we refer to the Machine Aesthetic of the twenties, we tend to forget how much of the symbolism of Modern architecture is based on industrial forms, if not industrial process, and how very obsolete this basis is. Everyone else knows the Industrial Revolution is dead. Why don't the architects? Is it not time for architects to connect with some new revolution, perhaps the electronic one? The existing commercial Strip with moving lights and signs involving representation and symbolism and meaning, and elements far apart in space to accommodate cars moving and parked, is as relevant to us now as were the factories with their industrial processes and functional programs several generations ago. Of course this conclusion is made with hindsight; as artists we found we liked the Strip before we analyzed why it seemed right.

SCARLATTI AND THE BEATLES

A connoisseur of music will pride himself on the catholicity of his taste. He will play for his friends, on the same evening, records of Scarlatti *and* the Beatles. Why will this person accept in his own living room, where you would expect him to be not at all tolerant of intrusions on his sensibilities, what he will not accept in the landscape? Why will he be outraged by the local commercial strip at the edge of town, support sign control in the belief that the way to limit bad architecture is to limit the size of signs, and confidently join the local design review board as an architectural connoisseur too? Why will he condemn pop architecture and accept pop music? That Scarlatti will live one thousand years and the Beatles only fifty years is beside the point, and he knows it; there is room for, and need for, a hierarchy of musical forms in our lives. Why not the same thing for architectural forms in our landscapes?

The answer is that our connoisseur clings to outmoded ideas about architecture as a whole. One of these ideas is that there is one dominant and correct canon of taste in our culture and that any art where this canon has not been followed is deviant and inferior. Herbert Gans has effectively countered this idea as a sociologist in his work on the relativity of taste and by his enumeration of the multiple taste cultures in our society; in most fields and media other than those of architecture the heterogeneous quality and ethnic diversity of American culture is accepted and is considered one of the strengths of our culture.

Other ideas which influence our connoisseur are promoted by Modern architects and they concern aesthetic unity: simple forms and pure order are the only good, and the architect (and later it would be the planner) will lead the community toward these goals. Gropius advocated "total design," but we are ending up with total control—total control through design review boards which promote high design, exclude popular architecture and in the process discourage quality in any architecture and stultify the diversity and hierarchy which have always been part of balanced and vital community architecture.

PLAIN AND FANCY ARCHITECTURE

As there is room for high design and popular art in the architecture of our communities, there is the need for plain and fancy styles of architecture. The strip, for instance, is the place not only for spectacular symbols, but also for conventional symbols. Most architectural complexes include hierarchies of architectural symbolism. They include original and special elements and conventional and ordinary elements—what we call plain and fancy styles—that are applied with a sense of appropriateness. The palazzo in an Italian town sits among its *contorni*—the name for the vegetables arranged beautifully around the meat in the serving platter at an important meal as well as for the plain architecture at the foot of fancy architecture. I am not advocating hierarchies based on a social caste system, but I am saying that an art school, for instance, is not a cathedral, and that most architecture in a normal context should be plain. Most Modern architects have tended to lose a sense of appropriateness in their urban renewal piazzas and in the often strident college campuses and towns where Modern architecture dominates. This is a plea for a symbolism of the ordinary in the ornament applied to shelter.

We have written, in *Learning from Las Vegas,* of our propensity as architects for modest architecture based at first on necessity, on our experience as a little firm with small jobs and limited budgets, then on an intuition that our situation had a general significance, and finally on a conviction that ours is not an era for heroic or pure architectural statements. Rhetoric for our landscape, when it is appropriate, will come from a less formal and more symbolic medium than pure architecture—perhaps from combinations of signs and sculpture and moving lights which decorate and represent. The source for our fancy architecture is in the conventions of the commercial strip. Its prototype is not the spatial Baroque monument, but the Early Christian basilica, that plain barn smothered in frescoes, the decorated shed par excellence. Ours is also not an era for expensive buildings: our national budgets do not support the architectural glories of a Parthenon or a Chartres, our collective heart is not in architecture, our collective values direct us in other paths, sometimes social, often military, and our technology and our labor systems promote standard systems of conventional construction.

These are our reasons for advocating and for trying to design shelter with decoration on it: shelter as a manifestation of systems building, conventional in its form and ordinary in its symbolism, always plain and never fancy. But also shelter as a grid for decoration—ordinary in its symbolism if a plain style is appropriate (and it usually is) and heroic in its symbolism if (and only if) a fancy style is appropriate. Function and structure can now go their own ways without regard to rhetoric, and our glories can come perhaps from mass housing, universal and efficient as a structural shelter, but parochial and diverse in its ornamental and symbolic appliqué. This is a way to be sensitive to the practical needs and the expressive wants of the many different people in the world.

Virtual Powers

Suzanne Langer

. . . The most widely accepted view is that the essence of dance is musical: the dancer expresses in gesture what he feels as the emotional content of the music which is the efficient and supporting cause of his dance. He reacts as we all would if we were not inhibited; his dance is self-expression, and is beautiful because the stimulus is beautiful. He may really be said to be "dancing the music."

This view of dance as a gestural rendering of musical forms is not merely a popular one, but is held by a great many dancers, and a few—though, indeed, very few—musicians. The music critic who calls himself Jean D'Udine has written, in his very provocative (not to say maddening) little book, *L'art et le geste:* "The expressive gesticulation of an orchestra conductor is simply a dance. . . . All music is dance—all melody just a series of attitudes, poses." Jacques Dalcroze, too, who was a musician and not a dancer by training, believed that dance could express in bodily movement the same motion-patterns that music creates for the ear. But as a rule it is the dancer, choreographer, or dance critic rather than the musician who regards dance as a musical art. On the assumption that all music could be thus "translated," Fokine undertook to dance Beethoven symphonies; Massine has done the same—both, apparently, with indifferent success.

Alexander Sakharoff, in his *Reflexions sur la musique et sur la danse,* carried the "musical" creed to its full length: "We—Clotilde Sakharoff and I—do not dance *to* music, or with musical accompaniment, we dance *the music.*" He reiterates the point several times. The person who taught him to dance not *with* music, but to dance the music itself, he says, was Isadora Duncan. There can be no doubt that she regarded dance as the visible incarnation of music—that for her there was no "dance music," but only pure music rendered as dance. Sakharoff remarked that many critics maintained Isadora did not really understand the music she danced, that she misinterpreted and violated it; he, on the contrary, found that she understood it so perfectly that she could dare to make free interpretations of it. Now, paradoxically, I believe both Sakharoff and the critics were right. Isadora did not understand the music *musically,* but for her purposes she understood it perfectly; she knew what was balletic, and that was all she knew about it. In fact, it was so absolutely all she knew that she thought it was all there was to know, and that what she danced was really "the music." Her musical taste as such was undeveloped—not simply poor, but utterly unaccountable. She ranked Ethelbert Nevin's "Narcissus" with Beethoven's C# Minor Sonata, and Mendelssohn's "Spring Song" with some very good Chopin *Etudes* her mother played. . . .

An excerpt

There is another interpretation of dance, inspired by the classical ballet, and therefore more generally accepted in the past than in our day: that dance is one of the plastic arts, a spectacle of shifting pictures, or animated design, or even statues in motion. Such was the opinion of the great choreographer Noverre who, of course, had never seen actual moving pictures or mobile sculpture. Since these media have come into existence, the difference between their products and dance is patent. Calder's balanced shapes, moved by the wind, define a truly sculptural volume which they fill with a free and fascinating motion (I am thinking, in particular, of his "Lobster Pot and Fishtail" in the stair well of the Museum of Modern Art in New York), but they certainly are not dancing. The moving picture has been seriously likened to the dance on the ground that both are "arts of movement"; yet the hypnotic influence of motion is really all they have in common (unless the film happens to be of a dance performance), and a peculiar psychological effect is not the measure of an art form. A screenplay, a newsreel, a documentary film, has no artistic similarity to any sort of dance.

Neither musical rhythm nor physical movement is enough to engender a dance. We speak of gnats "dancing" in the air, or balls "dancing" on a fountain that tosses them; but in reality all such patterned motions are *dance motifs,* not dances.

The same thing may be said of a third medium that has sometimes been regarded as the basic element in dance: pantomime. According to the protagonists of this view, dancing is a dramatic art. And of course they have a widely accepted theory, namely that Greek drama arose from choric dance, to justify their approach. But if one looks candidly at the most elaborate pantomimic dance, it does not appear at all like the action of true drama; one is far more tempted to doubt the venerable origins of acting than to believe in the dramatic ideal of dance motions. For dance that begins in pantomime, as many religious dances do, tends in the course of its subsequent history to become more balletic, not more dramatic. Pantomime, like pure motion patterns, plastic images, and musical forms, is dance material, something that may become a balletic element, but the dance itself is something else.

The true relationship is well stated by [Frank] Thiess, who regards pantomime itself as "a bastard of two different arts," namely dance and comedy, but observes: "To conclude from this fact that it [pantomime] is therefore condemned to eternal sterility, is to misapprehend the nature of some highly important formative processes in art. . . . A true dance pantomime may indeed be evolved, purely within the proper confines of the dance . . . a pantomime that is based entirely, from the first measure to the last, on the intrinsic law of the dance: the law of rhythmic motion." As the first master of such truly balletic miming he names Rudolf von Laban. "In his work," he says, "as in pure music, the content of an event disappears entirely behind its choreographic form. . . . Everything becomes expression, gesture, thrall and liberation of bodies. And by the skillful use of space and color, the balletic pantomime has been evolved, which may underlie the ensemble dance of the future."

What, then, is dance? If it be an independent art, as indeed it seems to be, it must have its own "primary illusion." Rhythmic motion? That is its actual process, not an illusion. The "primary illusion" of an art is something created, and created at the first touch—in this case, with the first motion, performed or even implied. The motion itself, as a physical reality and therefore "material" in the art, must suffer transformation. Into what?—Thiess, in the passage just quoted, has given the answer: "Everything becomes expression, *gesture*. . . ."

All dance motion is gesture, or an element in the exhibition of gesture—perhaps its mechanical contrast and foil, but always motivated by the semblance of an expressive movement. Mary Wigman has said, somewhere: "A meaningless gesture is abhorrent to me." Now a "meaningless gesture" is really a contradiction in terms; but to the great dancer all movement in dance was gesture—that was the only word; a mistake was a "meaningless gesture." The interesting point is that the statement itself might just as well have been made by Isadora Duncan, by Laban, or by Noverre. For, oddly enough, artists who hold the most fantastically diverse theories as to what dancing is—a visible music, a succession of pictures, an unspoken play—all recognize its gestic character. *Gesture* is the basic abstraction whereby the dance illusion is made and organized.

Gesture is vital movement; to the one who performs it, it is known very precisely as a kinetic experience, i.e. as action, and somewhat more vaguely by sight, as an effect. To others it appears as a visible motion, but not a motion of things, sliding or waving or rolling around—it is *seen and understood* as vital movement. So it is always at once subjective and objective, personal and public, willed (or evoked) and perceived.

In actual life gestures function as signals or symptoms of our desires, intentions, expectations, demands, and feelings. Because they can be consciously controlled, they may also be elaborated, just like vocal sounds, into a system of assigned and combinable *symbols*, a genuine discursive language. People who do not understand each other's speech always resort to this simpler form of discourse to express propositions, questions, judgments. But whether a gesture has linguistic meaning or not, it is always spontaneously expressive, too, by virtue of its form: it is free and big, or nervous and tight, quick or leisurely, etc., according to the psychological condition of the person who makes it. This self-expressive aspect is akin to the tone of voice in speech.

Gesticulation, as part of our actual behavior, is not art. It is simply vital movement. A squirrel, startled, sitting up with its paw against its heart, makes a gesture, and a very expressive one at that. But there is no art in its behavior. It is not dancing. Only when the movement that was a genuine gesture in the squirrel is *imagined*, so it may be performed apart from the squirrel's momentary situation and mentality, it becomes an artistic element, a possible dance-gesture. Then it becomes a free symbolic form, which may be used to convey *ideas* of emotion, of awareness and premonition, or may be combined with or incorporated in other virtual gestures, to express other physical and mental tensions.

Every being that makes natural gestures is a center of vital force, and its expressive movements are seen by others as signals of its will. But virtual gestures are not signals, they are symbols of will. The spontaneously gestic character of dance motions is illusory, and the vital force they express is illusory; the "powers" (i.e. centers of vital force) in dance are created beings—created by the semblance gesture.

The primary illusion of dance is a virtual realm of Power—not actual, physically exerted power, but appearances of influence and agency created by virtual gesture.

In watching a collective dance—say, an artistically successful ballet—one does not see *people running around;* one sees the dance driving this way, drawn that way, gathering here, spreading there—fleeing, resting, rising, and so forth; and all the motion seems to spring from powers beyond the performers. In a *pas de deux* the two dancers appear to magnetize each other; the relation between them is more than a spatial one, it is a relation of forces; but the forces they exercise, that seem to be as physical as those which orient the compass needle toward its pole, really do not exist physically at all. They are dance forces, virtual powers.

The prototype of these purely apparent energies is not the "field of forces" known to physics, but the subjective experience of volition and free agency, and of reluctance to alien, compelling wills. The consciousness of life, the sense of vital power, even of the power to receive impressions, apprehend the environment, and meet changes, is our most immediate self-consciousness. This is the feeling of power; and the play of such "felt" energies is as different from any system of physical forces as psychological time is from clock-time, and psychological space from the space of geometry.

The widely popular doctrine that every work of art takes rise from an emotion which agitates the artist, and which is directly "expressed" in the work, may be found in the literature of every art. That is why scholars delve into each famous artist's life history, to learn by discursive study what emotions he must have had while making this or that piece, so that they may "understand" the message of the work. But there are usually a few philosophical critics—sometimes artists themselves—who realize that the feeling in a work of art is something the artist *conceived* as he created the symbolic form to present it, rather than something he was undergoing and involuntarily venting in an artistic process. There is a Wordsworth who finds that poetry is not a symptom of emotional stress, but an image of it—"emotion recollected in tranquility"; there is a Riemann who recognizes that music *resembles* feeling, and is its objective symbol rather than its physiological effect; a Mozart who knows from experience that emotional disturbance merely interferes with artistic conception. Only in the literature of the dance, the claim to direct self-expression is very nearly unanimous. Not only the sentimental Isadora, but such eminent theorists as Merle Armitage and Rudolf von Laban, and scholars like Curt Sachs, besides countless dancers judging introspectively, accept the naturalistic doctrine that dance is a free discharge either of surplus energy or of emotional excitement.

Confronted with such evidence, one naturally is led to reconsider the whole theory of art as symbolic form. Is dance an exception? Good theories may have special cases, but not exceptions. Does the whole philosophy break down? Does it simply not "work" in the case of dance, and thereby reveal a fundamental weakness that was merely obscurable in other contexts? Surely no one would have the temerity to claim that *all* the experts on a subject are wrong!

Now there is one curious circumstance, which points the way out of this quandary: namely, that the really great experts—choreographers, dancers, aestheticians, and historians—although explicitly they assert the emotive-symptom thesis, implicitly contradict it when they talk about any particular dance or any specified process. No one, to my knowledge, has ever maintained that Pavlova's rendering of slowly ebbing life in "The Dying Swan" was most successful when she actually felt faint and sick, or proposed to put Mary Wigman into the proper mood for her tragic "Evening Dances" by giving her a piece of terrible news a few minutes before she entered on the stage. A good ballet master, wanting a ballerina to register dismay, might say: "Imagine that your boyfriend has just eloped with your most trusted chum!" But he would not say, with apparent seriousness, "Your boyfriend told me to tell you goodby from him, he's not coming to see you any more." Or he might suggest to a sylph rehearsing a "dance of joy" that she should fancy herself on a vacation in California, amid palms and orange groves, but he probably would not remind her of an exciting engagement after the rehearsal, because that would distract her from the dance, perhaps even to the point of inducing false motions.

It is *imagined feeling* that governs the dance, not real emotional conditions. If one passes over the spontaneous emotion theory with which almost every modern book on the dance begins, one quickly comes to the evidence for this contention. Dance gesture is not real gesture, but virtual. The bodily movement, of course, is real enough; but *what makes it emotive gesture,* i.e. its spontaneous origin in what Laban calls a "feeling-thought-motion," is illusory, so the movement is "gesture" only within the dance. It is *actual movement,* but *virtual self-expression. . . .*